SPORTS HEROES AND LEGENDS™

Doug Flutie

Read all of the books in this exciting,
action-packed biography series!

Hank Aaron	Wayne Gretzky
Muhammad Ali	Derek Jeter
Lance Armstrong	Sandy Koufax
David Beckham	Michelle Kwan
Barry Bonds	Mickey Mantle
Roberto Clemente	Jesse Owens
Sasha Cohen	Alex Rodriguez
Joe DiMaggio	Wilma Rudolph
Tim Duncan	Annika Sorenstam
Dale Earnhardt Jr.	Ichiro Suzuki
Doug Flutie	Jim Thorpe
Lou Gehrig	Tiger Woods

SPORTS HEROES AND LEGENDS™

Doug Flutie

by Matt Doeden

TFCB Twenty-First Century Books/Minneapolis

For Gina

Twenty-First Century Books
A division of Lerner Publishing Group, Inc.
241 First Avenue North
Minneapolis, MN 55401 U.S.A.

Website address: www.lernerbooks.com

Cover photograph:
© David Stluka/Getty Images

Library of Congress Cataloging-in-Publication Data

Doeden, Matt.
     Doug Flutie / by Matt Doeden.
        p.   cm. — (Sports heroes and legends)
     Includes bibliographical references and index.
     ISBN-13: 978-0-8225-7162-9 (lib. bdg. : alk. paper)
     1. Flutie, Doug—Juvenile literature. 2. Football players—United States—
Biography—Juvenile literature. 3. Canadian Football League—Juvenile
literature. 4. Buffalo Bills (Football team)—Juvenile literature. I. Title.
GV939.F59D64 2008
796.332092—dc22   2006029859
     [B]

Manufactured in the United States of America
1 2 3 4 5 6 – JR – 13 12 11 10 09 08

Contents

Prologue

The Pass

The game was a mismatch in every sense of the word. On November 23, 1984, quarterback Doug Flutie led his Boston College Eagles onto the field to face the Miami Hurricanes. Doug was one of college football's best quarterbacks, and the Eagles were a top-10 team. But experts gave the Eagles little chance to defeat the mighty Miami Hurricanes.

The Hurricanes were the defending national champions. They were almost unbeatable in their home stadium, the Orange Bowl. Their quarterback, Bernie Kosar, was a classic, 6-foot-5 passer. Strong, smart, and accurate, Kosar was clearly headed to the National Football League (NFL) after college. Meanwhile, Boston College had Doug Flutie, a scrappy scrambler who stood just 5 foot 9 and weighed a mere 176 pounds. Lining up against Miami's big, fearsome defense, Doug looked more like a ball boy than a top quarterback.

1

Many people expected the Hurricanes to blow the Eagles and their undersized quarterback out of the stadium. But Doug had spent his whole career hearing about what he shouldn't—and couldn't—do. Criticism hadn't stopped him before, and it wouldn't stop him this time.

The Eagles soon silenced the noisy Miami crowd. The spectators looked on in disbelief as the Eagles took the opening kickoff and drove through wind and rain to take an early 7–0 lead. The disbelief only grew on the Eagles' next possession, when Doug led them to another touchdown and a 14–0 lead. Doug had thrown eleven passes, and he'd completed every one of them.

The Hurricanes were the defending national champions for a reason, though. Kosar matched Doug's feat by completing his next eleven passes and leading his team to two scores. Just like that, Miami had stormed back to tie the game, 14–14.

The game became an offensive slugfest. The two quarterbacks succeeded with vastly different styles. Kosar was cool and efficient. He executed play after play, exactly according to the coaches' plans. He calmly surveyed the field, found his receivers, and used crisp, clean passes. Doug, meanwhile, was always a bit frantic, always hanging on the edge of control. At the slightest defensive pressure, he'd bound toward the sidelines, creating new plays on the run.

The styles may have been very different, but the results were similar. By halftime, Doug and the Eagles held a 28–21 lead. But a 7-point lead was far from safe. The fireworks continued in the second half. The teams went back and forth, with neither side able to pull away to a big lead. With about three minutes left, Boston College scored to take a 41–38 lead. Kosar led the Hurricane offense onto the field for what looked like the game's final drive.

At first, Boston's defense stood tall. After a penalty, Miami was backed up into a tough third-and-21 hole (third down, 21 yards to go for a first down), deep in their own end of the field. Kosar took the snap and dropped back. An Eagle defender flew at his face, but he ducked the tackle and completed a 20-yard pass downfield.

The completion set up a fourth-and-1 play. If Miami couldn't gain a yard, Boston College would take the ball. The game would be all but over. But the Hurricanes made it, and their hopes stayed alive.

The confident Kosar continued to complete his passes. Miami moved closer and closer to the Boston College end zone. As the clock ticked under a minute, Kosar completed a screen (a short pass behind blockers) to Eddie Brown, who powered his way inside the 5-yard line. Finally, with just 28 seconds left, running back Melvin Bratton punched it in for the touchdown. After the extra point, Miami led 45–41. The crowd went crazy. The players on the Miami sideline celebrated.

The Miami touchdown was like a punch in the gut for the players on the Boston College sideline. Safety Dave Pereira said, "The only thought I had was that we just lost the game."

Doug knew the Eagles were in trouble. They had just 28 seconds to drive 80 yards down the field and score a touchdown. A field goal, for 3 points, would do them no good. Winning was the longest of long shots, but Doug wasn't going to let his teammates give up. In the huddle, he told them, "We can do it. No mistakes."

After a holding penalty against Miami on the drive's first play, only 20 seconds remained. The end zone was still a long way away. On the next play, Doug scrambled and found receiver Troy Stradford, who was tackled at the Miami 48-yard line. Doug wanted to make another 20 to 30 yards to set up a final play. But his pass to tight end Peter Casparriello sailed long, incomplete. The Eagles, still at midfield, had only 6 seconds left. That was time for just one more play. It had to be a Hail Mary, a long desperation pass to the end zone.

Doug knew what to do. Every receiver would run to the end zone, and Doug would heave the ball as far as he could. Boston College fans could only hope that Doug would throw it far enough and that an Eagles player would come down with it.

The Hurricanes knew what was coming. With extra defensive backs in the game, they would all drop back to guard against the Hail Mary. Doug took the snap from center. He waited as his receivers streaked down the field. A Miami defender broke through the Boston College offensive line and tried to tackle Doug, but the little quarterback dropped back farther and slipped away. The final seconds were ticking off the clock. By the time he was ready to throw, Doug had backed up all the way to Boston College's 38-yard line. He hurled the ball with all his strength.

The ball sailed in a long, high arc. It seemed to just hang in the air for a few seconds. As it approached the end zone, two Miami defenders collided as they tried to knock it down. Suddenly, Gerald Phelan—Doug's roommate—was open. With his feet in the end zone, Phelan caught the ball against his chest. He clung to it as he fell to the ground. As he got up and stood with the ball in his hands, the referee made the signal: *touchdown.*

Phelan was shocked. The crowd and Hurricane players were stunned. And more than 60 yards away, Doug still wasn't sure exactly what had happened—the taller linemen in front of him blocked his view. At first, he thought the pass had fallen incomplete. He barely believed it when he finally saw the touchdown signal.

Against all odds, Boston College had won, 47–45. The celebration was on. An excited Doug jumped into the arms of his linemen.

"That wasn't Gerald Phelan who caught the ball," Boston College guard Mark MacDonald said after the game. "God caught that ball."

Lineman Jim Ostrowski overheard the comment. "No," he said. "God threw it." The legend of Doug Flutie, football's classic underdog, was born.

Chapter One

A Love of Sports

Born October 23, 1962, in Manchester, Maryland, Douglas Richard Flutie had sports in his blood. His older brother and sister, Bill and Denise, both played and watched sports. Later, his younger brother, Darren, would share the same passion. His parents, Richard and Joan, always supported their children's love of athletics.

Some of Doug's earliest memories were of watching the Baltimore Colts football team and Baltimore Orioles baseball team with his dad. He was fascinated by almost any sport, and the only thing better than watching a game was playing one. Whether it was football, baseball, basketball, or something completely made up, Doug wanted to compete. Even inside on a rainy day, Doug was always making up new games.

"Doug always had to be playing," said Bill. "He used to make up games, and they were serious games. Hall football.

Cup baseball—crush a snow-cone cup, hit it with your hand, and go around the bases."

When Doug was six, the family moved from Maryland to Melbourne, Florida. The state's year-round warm weather suited Doug perfectly—he could spend even more time outside. At Gemini Elementary School, Doug and Bill played every sport they could. Neither of their parents were experienced athletes, but they always encouraged their children. Richard volunteered to coach their Little League teams. Joan often coached girls' teams. She helped raise money for the teams by selling snacks at games.

Richard Flutie, Doug's dad, worked as an engineer. But his first love was music. He led his own jazz band and made sure all his children appreciated music. As adults, Doug learned to play drums and Darren learned guitar. They got together with other musicians and formed their own rock-and-roll band, the Flutie Brothers Band. The group even recorded two CDs.

The family wasn't rich, but they had enough to get by. Richard and Joan sent the children to sports camps and made sure they had all the equipment they needed. "[My father] was excellent in helping us," Doug later said. "Whenever we needed something athletically, he was always there. He wanted to be a part of whatever we were a part of. And that really helped us all along and got us going."

Richard built the boys their own pitching mound and plate in the family's backyard. There, Doug spent hours practicing his pitching, trying to throw strikes. When he and Bill grew tired of throwing a baseball, they'd throw a football.

By age nine, Doug was playing organized youth football. But there was a problem. The league had a weight restriction of 68 pounds. Boys lighter than that weren't allowed in the league. Doug weighed just 63 pounds. The coaches broke the rule and let him be on the team but would play him only on kickoffs. They didn't think he could handle regular plays with the heavier boys.

In time, Doug played his way onto the field despite his size. The coaches used him as a defensive back, a position for which speed counts more than size. Doug would rather have played quarterback. But that position was locked down by his older brother. Bill was a great athlete and would go on to make the league's all-star team.

The constant sports and roughhousing took a toll on Doug's body. At nine he broke his finger wrestling. When he was twelve, he broke his foot playing football with his younger brother, Darren. In a Little League game, he took a ball to the face and broke his nose. But none of the injuries dimmed his love of sports. As soon as he recovered, he was back out playing.

In 1976 Doug's days of playing in the Florida sun ended. He was thirteen when the family moved to Natick, Massachusetts, outside Boston. Because of his love of sports, fitting in at a new school was no problem for Doug. At the time, Bill was the family's football star. Doug's favorite sport was basketball. Because he was small and quick, he played point guard. The point guard handles the ball and directs the other players on the court, somewhat like a quarterback in football.

> ❝I had friends at school, but my closest friends were the athletes I played with. On the Little League field or basketball court, we were all in the same circle. Our interests rubbed off on each other and we became friends.❞
>
> —Doug Flutie

Although basketball was Doug's passion, he also played baseball and football. In baseball, he was a pitcher and a shortstop. On his junior high football team, he finally got a chance to play quarterback. His coach, Kirk Buschenfeldt, recognized something special in Doug. "Not only was he a tremendous athlete, but he had the brains to go along with it," the coach

10

said. "Instead of always reacting to situations, he was always anticipating situations, and his reactions were so much more on the mark because of that."

Buschenfeldt had so much faith in Doug that he even let him call his own plays. That's unusual at any level of football but almost unheard of for a player so young.

In the fall of 1978, Doug entered tenth grade and earned a spot on the Natick High School varsity football team. Bill, a senior, was the team's quarterback. Doug returned to his old spot as a defensive back.

Despite standing just 5 foot 8 and weighing only 150 pounds, Doug was an important part of the team. In the season's first game, he blitzed (rushed at) the opposing quarterback. After getting around a blocker, he found himself in a pile of bigger players. The quarterback had fumbled, and everyone tried to get the ball. Somehow Doug got his hands on the ball and took off running. His fumble recovery and runback led to a Natick touchdown—the only points of the game.

Natick won its next two games as well, but the team had a problem. The defense was playing great, but the offense was struggling. When the team lost its fourth game, 8–6, Coach Tom Lamb was ready to make a change at quarterback.

He thought about switching one Flutie with another. But first, he wanted a good look at Doug's quarterbacking skills. So he had Doug play for Natick's junior varsity team for one game. Doug led Natick to 52 points and a win. Lamb's decision was made—Doug was the new varsity quarterback. Bill, meanwhile, would move to wide receiver.

Doug was always changing plays on the run. That made him difficult to predict and exciting to watch. "Watching Doug was always a thrill," said Doug's mom. "Bill, our oldest son, always did very well. He got the play done. But . . . it would still be more fun to watch Doug play."

Doug's first game at quarterback was against Milton High School. At the start, Lamb must have questioned his decision. Doug began terribly, throwing four interceptions in the first half alone. But the coaches stuck with Doug, and he rewarded them by throwing three touchdowns (all to Bill) and winning the game.

Doug did more than just lead the offense that year. He was also the team's kicker. In the final game of the year against Braintree High School, he kicked a 38-yard field goal with 3 seconds left on the clock. The kick gave Natick a 27–25 victory. It was a great way to finish off the season.

With the football season over, Doug turned his attention to other activities. He got good grades, and he earned a spot on the school's varsity basketball and baseball teams. He started dating classmate Laurie Fortier. Soon the two were inseparable. Laurie was a big sports fan and always cheered Doug on from the stands.

Not everything was perfect, though. The Fluties were having money troubles. In the spring of 1979, sixteen-year-old Doug quit the Natick baseball team to take a job at an ice cream stand. He wanted to make his own money instead of having to ask his parents for it.

After high school, Bill Flutie went to Brown University, where he played wide receiver for the football team.

Over the next two years, Doug continued to excel both in the classroom and in sports. During his senior year, college football coaches began to recruit him. He would have preferred to play college basketball, but with his small size, major basketball programs weren't interested in him.

His size also limited his football options. Many college coaches liked his athletic ability, but they didn't think he was big enough to be a successful college quarterback. One coach told him, "Let's face it, you're not going to be a quarterback at the Division I level [DI—the top college level]. You're a good athlete. You might be a defensive back; you might be a wide receiver."

HIGH SCHOOL HONORS

Doug was one of the top high school athletes in Massachusetts. He was named a state all-star in basketball. In football, he was twice named to the *Boston Globe* all-star team—once as a defensive back, once as a quarterback.

Doug's best offers came from Division I-AA schools (one level below DI) such as Holy Cross and the University of New Hampshire. Jack Bicknell, at the DI-AA University of Maine, also recruited Doug. Then Bicknell took over the coaching job at Boston College (BC), a DI school. Bicknell still wanted Doug. When BC's top two quarterback recruits decided to attend college elsewhere, Bicknell offered Doug one of the program's few remaining scholarships (money to pay for school). Doug accepted. He was thrilled to be playing for a DI school, and Boston College was near his family home in Natick.

That summer, Doug had one last game to play before he started his college career. He was picked for the Massachusetts high school all-star game, to be held at Boston College. In the game, he led his team, which was an underdog, to a big win. For his efforts, he took home the game's Most Valuable Player (MVP) trophy.

The award was an excellent way to impress his new BC coaches, who were on hand to watch the game. "You could see he was absolutely in control of that game," Bicknell said of Doug's performance. "He just took over. I said that night, 'We're not going to be moving him from quarterback.'" With that, Doug was ready for college.

Chapter | Two

BC Eagle

When Doug reported to BC for football practice in the fall of 1981, his coaches weren't quite sure what to do with him. Everyone agreed that he was a great athlete and had great quarterbacking skills. But at 5 foot 9, he just didn't look like a quarterback. Coaches wondered if he'd even be able to see over the top of his big offensive linemen. When he first started practice, he was about eighth on the team's quarterback depth chart (meaning there were seven quarterbacks in line to play before him). That was a long way down, and Doug thought about switching positions in hopes of playing sooner. "I had convinced myself that I wasn't going to be a quarterback," he said. "I thought I'd be a defensive back or a split end. It didn't matter as long as I could play major college football."

With good play and a few injuries to other players, Doug had moved up to fourth string by the start of the season. Then the starter, John Loughery, got hurt. The other two quarterbacks in front of Doug took turns leading the BC offense, but both struggled badly. The Eagles were blown out three games in a row. Coach Bicknell was embarrassed, and he was growing desperate. It seemed that nothing he did would fix BC's terrible offense.

EAGLE WOES

Boston College had one of the country's lowliest football programs when Doug started school in 1981. They'd gone 0–11 just three seasons before and were often one of the worst teams in the National Collegiate Athletic Association (NCAA). Worse still, they hadn't been to a bowl (postseason) game since 1943.

In the team's fourth game, they played the powerful Penn State University (PSU) Nittany Lions, one of the nation's best teams. Again, it was a blowout. By the fourth quarter, 85,000 PSU fans were partying and celebrating their team's 38–0 lead. BC's offense couldn't move the football. The BC coaches had nothing to lose, so they told Doug to get ready.

Doug could barely believe he was getting a chance. "I had so much nervous energy it was ridiculous," he said. He could hardly remember the plays.

He entered the game on BC's own 22-yard line. After a pair of running plays, Doug finally threw his first pass—a 15-yard completion for a first down. The first down gave the team a much-needed confidence boost. Mixing the run and the pass, Doug and the Eagles continued to drive the ball downfield. Finally, Doug threw a 23-yard completion to Scott Nizolek in the back left corner of the end zone for a touchdown.

> ❝[Doug] just made everyone around him play better and it was obvious that he was the guy.❞
>
> —COACH JACK BICKNELL

With a 78-yard scoring drive and three completions in three throws, Doug had saved his team from an embarrassing shutout. On BC's next possession, Doug almost scored again. He took the offense all the way down to PSU's 2-yard line before throwing an interception in the end zone. The Eagles lost the game 38–7, but they'd found a quarterback.

In just one quarter, Doug had completed eight passes for 135 yards. More important, he'd done what no other BC quarterback had been able to do that year—move the offense. "It was like somebody hit a switch and the tempo picked up,"

18

Bicknell said of Doug's influence on the offense. "Never, ever could we imagine what we had [in Doug Flutie]."

Still, Doug was a freshman quarterback playing one of the nation's toughest schedules. He was just nineteen. Some growing pains were to be expected. One of them happened the next week, when Navy thumped the Eagles 25–10.

Through five games, BC had scored a miserable 54 points. If they wanted to compete, the offense had to do a lot better. To say it improved in the sixth game, against Army, would be an understatement. The Eagles jumped out to a 27–0 lead and went on to win 41–6. Doug went 15 for 21 (fifteen completions in twenty-one pass attempts) for 244 yards and three touchdowns.

The win boosted the team's confidence. Their next opponent was the nation's number-2 team, the Pittsburgh Panthers. The nation's best college quarterback, Dan Marino, led the powerful Panther attack.

As expected, Pitt jumped out to an early lead, 29–10. But Doug and his teammates kept fighting. An 88-yard drive in the third quarter pulled the Eagles to within 12 points. They scored again on the next drive, cutting the margin to 29–24.

It was a stunning turn of events. Pitt was the vastly better team, but somehow the little freshman quarterback had kept BC in the game. Late in the fourth quarter, he had his offense at

Pitt's 8-yard line, with a chance to take the lead. But a fumble gave the Panthers the ball back.

Undaunted, the Eagle defense forced a punt, giving the offense another chance. Once again, Doug and the offense moved the ball deep into Pitt territory. They reached the 9-yard line before a penalty and a sack forced a field goal attempt (which missed). BC never got another shot, and Pitt held on for the 29–24 victory. In the loss, Doug was 23 for 42 with 347 yards passing and two touchdowns. If a team could ever feel good about a loss, this was the time. The Eagles were no longer a laughingstock. With Doug under center, they always believed they had a chance.

Doug started each of BC's final four games. The team won three of them, losing only to Syracuse, a loss in which Doug was sacked eight times. The team's final record of 5–6 didn't look great, but they'd exceeded expectations and finally had some hope going into the 1982 season.

While football was always first on Doug's mind—even in the off-season—he also focused on his studies. He majored in computer programming. He worked hard to learn how to write and test computer programs. He also continued to date Laurie. The couple was very serious and already making plans for their future together. But Doug's highest priority was football. It was his passion, and he couldn't wait to return to the field for his sophomore season.

As tough as 1981 had been, 1982 looked to be even more challenging. Experts rated BC's schedule as the fifth-toughest in the nation. The Eagles, still a young team, had their work cut out for them.

The team wasted little time in proving they were up to the challenge. In the opening game—on the road against a top-20 team, Texas A&M—Doug and the Eagles surprised everyone with a blowout victory. They led 24–6 at the half and cruised to a 38–16 win. Doug led the charge, going 18 for 26 for 356 yards and three touchdowns.

&&He believes in everything he does. He's flipping the ball around, doing some really goofy things . . . and they work. You watch him and just hope you don't coach all that [talent] out of him.&&

—COACH JACK BICKNELL

The next week, Clemson—the defending national champion—jumped out to a 14–0 lead. But in classic Doug Flutie style, the Eagles came back, tying the game at 17 in the fourth quarter. At the time, college football had no overtime, so when neither team scored again, the game ended in a tie. Considering the top-level opponent, a tie was a fantastic result for BC. But

Doug wasn't happy. "A tie is all right," he said. "But we should have won that game. We had our chances."

Doug may not have been impressed, but with the win over Texas A&M and the tie with Clemson, the team and its quarterback made national headlines. Newspaper reporters wanted to interview the sophomore sensation. TV stations ran stories about the underdog Eagles. All the recruiters who had overlooked Doug as he searched for a DI scholarship were noticing him this time.

After destroying Navy 31–0 and Temple 17–7, the Eagles were 3–0–1 and had climbed into the Associated Press's list of the top-20 college teams. They appeared to be on their way to BC's first bowl (postseason) game in more than forty years. But all the good feelings came crashing down the next week at West Virginia. Doug hurt his thumb early in the game and played terribly. He went 9 for 33 and threw four interceptions. BC took its first loss of the year, 20–13.

Doug and the team didn't play much better against Rutgers the next week. But luckily, one of Doug's passes bounced off a defender's helmet and into the arms of the diving Gerald Phelan. Thanks in big part to that play, BC got a much-needed 20–13 win.

After beating Army, BC's record stood at 5–1–1. The next game was at home against Penn State—the last big challenge on the schedule. If the Eagles hoped to get into one of the top bowl games, they'd need a strong showing against the Nittany Lions.

A record crowd of more than 33,000 packed into BC's Alumni Stadium for the big game. Doug and the Eagle offense had an up-and-down game. On the good side, Doug completed a jaw-dropping 520 yards in passing—the highest single-game total of any college quarterback that year. But BC also commited six turnovers, including two Flutie interceptions, and had trouble scoring to finish off long drives. Because of those troubles, PSU easily won the game, 52–17.

At the time, Doug's total 520 passing yards against Penn State ranked as the tenth-highest passing total in NCAA history.

After the disappointing loss, BC won its final two regular-season games and earned an invitation to the Tangerine Bowl. It wasn't a famous bowl game, but the invitation was still a huge accomplishment for the team. After forty years of frustration, the Eagles were finally headed to postseason play.

The team traveled to Orlando, Florida, to meet their opponent, the Auburn Tigers. For Doug, the trip felt like going home again. He'd spent much of his childhood in Florida and was excited to be back.

Early in the game, Doug was nervous. He struggled, going 10 for 22 as Auburn jumped out to a 23–10 lead. This time, there was no BC comeback. Even a last-second touchdown and two-point conversion (putting the ball in the end zone for two points instead of kicking it for one point) left them short, 33–26. The loss was a disappointing end to the season.

WORKING MAN

In the summer of 1983, Doug and several other BC football players took jobs replacing the artificial turf on Alumni Field at Boston College. The job paid about $10 per hour, which was a good wage at the time. But Doug described the work as backbreaking and was happy when the job was finally done.

Doug and his teammates could still feel good about all they'd accomplished. They'd gone 8–3–1 against a tough schedule and had finished the season ranked 25th in the nation. That record wasn't bad for a team that had been one of the worst in college football less than two years before.

While athletically Doug was exceeding all expectations, he was having a hard time in the classroom. Early on, his grades had been good. But he later got lazy. He cut classes and skipped assignments. He showed little interest in learning. Football, not school, was his passion. Quarterback coach Tom Coughlin worried about his star player. He told Doug to get his academics in order. Just sliding by wasn't good enough, Coughlin said, especially if Doug didn't make it as a professional football player. Doug listened, worked harder, and even settled on a new major—speech communications. He was already thinking about a possible future as a broadcaster.

But that was a long way off. For the time being, Doug was a football player.

Chapter Three

Upperclassman

Interest in BC football was at an all-time high as the fall of 1983 approached. Ticket sales soared, newspapers ran more stories than ever on the team, and TV networks scrambled to get BC games on the air. The focus for all the coverage was always the team's unlikely star quarterback.

The season started with a personal milestone for Doug. In the first game, against Morgan State, he broke the BC career passing record (Frank Harris had owned the earlier record with 4,555 yards). But Morgan State, a Division II team, was just a warm-up. The season really began the next week against Clemson, a team hungry for revenge after BC had beaten them the year before. Clemson was so determined to contain Doug that its coach joked about using a "ten-man rush on Flutie," which meant he'd use ten of his eleven defenders just to stop Doug.

As expected, Clemson came out with fire. Their determination helped them jump to a 13–3 halftime lead. That lead grew to 16–3 in the third quarter, and it looked like Clemson would have its revenge. But then, in typical Boston College fashion, the Eagles came roaring back. Using a heavy running attack, Doug led the Eagles to four straight touchdowns and a 31–16 win.

In 1983 *Sports Illustrated* published a big story on Doug. He was pictured on the magazine's cover with the story title "A Little Man on Campus." It was the first time a BC athlete had ever been featured on the magazine's cover.

The comeback got Doug even more national attention. The NBC television network named him Sportsman of the Week. He appeared on the network's *Today* show and also did national TV interviews with CBS and ABC. Americans loved an underdog and a comeback, and Doug represented both.

With talk of a possible New Year's Day bowl game (at the time, the major college bowls were all played on January 1), the team kept rolling. They trounced Rutgers, despite losing Doug in the first half with a concussion (bruise to the brain). The only bump in the road was a 27–17 loss to the number-12-ranked West Virginia Mountaineers.

By late October, the Eagles were 5–1 and ranked 19th in the nation. Next up was the game they'd all been waiting for—Penn State. After being blown out in each of the last two years, the BC players badly wanted to beat the Nittany Lions, who had won the national title the year before.

Before a national TV audience, Doug and the Eagles got off to a fast start. On the game's first possession, they drove the ball 80 yards for a touchdown. BC extended the lead to 14–0 on the next drive and never looked back, winning 27–17. Beating PSU was a huge confidence boost. "Penn State!" Doug exclaimed as he celebrated the win. "We're on a level with Penn State!"

Again, talk turned to hopes of a New Year's Day bowl game. BC needed to keep playing well to impress bowl officials and earn a good invitation. But after a win against Army, the team's bowl hopes took a big hit in mid-November. BC suffered with a surprising 21–10 loss to Syracuse. Doug had a terrible game as well, going 12 for 36.

"I have to keep telling people that [Doug] is just a kid," Coach Bicknell said in defense of his young quarterback. As good as he usually was, even the twenty-one-year-old Doug was going to have bad days.

Doug and the team bounced back from the loss, winning their final two games. One of the wins was a nationally televised game against number-13 Alabama. BC's 9–2 record was good, but not good enough for a New Year's Day bowl. Instead, the team accepted an invitation to the Liberty Bowl in Memphis, Tennessee.

BLACKOUT BOWL

BC's 1983 win over Alabama was one of the most interesting games of Doug's college career. With the score tied 6–6 in the first half, a storm knocked out power to the stadium, leaving the scoreboard, clock, TV cameras, and everything else without power. But the game went on. At halftime, the Eagles gathered in the dark in the locker room. Power was finally restored in the second half, and the Eagles went on to a 20–13 win.

They would face the Notre Dame Fighting Irish. Notre Dame was traditionally a great team, but they had stumbled to a 6–5 record in 1983. They had been selected for the Liberty Bowl mainly because of their huge nationwide popularity, not because they'd played well enough to deserve the reward. BC was a heavy favorite to win the game. BC's coaches felt that a convincing win over Notre Dame would give the Eagles, then ranked 13th, a good chance at a top-10 finish.

Before the bowl season starts, the Downtown Athletic Club in New York City awards college football's highest individual honor, the Heisman Trophy. Doug was named a finalist for the trophy and attended the award ceremony. Nebraska's Mike Rozier won the award, but Doug was honored just to be included with the other finalists—Rozier and Brigham Young University's Steve Young.

The weather for the Liberty Bowl was icy and cold. The field was frozen solid, but the action was intense. Doug led the Eagles to an early touchdown. But the kicker, struggling with the cold and wind, missed the extra point. Notre Dame used a strong running attack to dominate the BC defense. The Irish went on long, time-consuming drives, a style that kept the ball out of Doug's hands. Soon, Notre Dame had a 19–6 lead.

Just before halftime, Doug struck again. The Eagles were at the Notre Dame 28-yard line, and Doug was ready to run a play for Gerald Phelan. "[Doug] looked at me and he was smiling [and] nodding his head," Phelan said. The wide receiver knew that if he could beat his defender, Doug would get him the ball.

Sure enough, the play went as planned. Phelan cut inside, Doug found him with a perfect pass, and the score was 19–12.

Not trusting his kicker, Bicknell chose to go for a 2-point conversion. But it failed, leaving the Eagles down by 7.

Despite suffering a hip injury in the second half, Doug led the offense for one more touchdown. Bicknell again chose the two-point conversion, even though an extra point would have tied the game. Again, the conversion failed, leaving BC down 19–18, a score that held up. For the second straight year, the Eagles had lost a bowl game.

Traditionally, a bowl game's MVP award goes to a member of the winning team. But Doug's three-touchdown performance had been so impressive that he earned the award even though his team had lost. The award was little consolation for the junior quarterback. He had wanted to win a bowl game.

He'd have one more chance to do that. Doug's senior season in 1984 would be unlike any before. He was a leading Heisman candidate. NFL scouts would be watching him closely. And for the first time since Doug and Bill had played together on the Natick High football team, Doug wouldn't be the only Flutie on the roster. His younger brother, Darren, had accepted a scholarship to BC and would join the team as a freshman wide receiver. "I remember thinking when he signed his scholarship offer that I just wanted him to get in a game so I could throw one pass to him for a completion," Doug later wrote in his autobiography.

Early in the season, all the talk was about Doug. Could he win the Heisman? Could he finally lead his team to a New Year's Day bowl? Could he get his first postseason victory?

Doug knew that the questions about winning and the questions about the Heisman were linked. Heisman voters tend to give the award to a player on one of the nation's top teams. "The Heisman is going to be determined by our won-lost record," he said. "If we're 8–3 or 7–4, I won't win. If we're 11–0 or 10–1, I'll be in the running."

The season started with a 44–24 win over Division I-AA Western Carolina. Then came the first big test: a road game against 9th-ranked Alabama, nicknamed the Crimson Tide. Before the game, Alabama's coach told a reporter that Doug was too short to succeed in the NFL. The coach said that Doug would make a great Canadian Football League quarterback, however.

As the game began, Doug and the Eagles showed few signs that they could repeat their 1983 victory over Alabama. The Crimson Tide dominated the first half, 24–14. That lead swelled to 31–14 in the third quarter. "It got real quiet on the bench," Doug said. "But there was still a lot of time."

Alabama felt so secure that its coaches started pulling starters out of the game. They even used their second-string quarterback. It was a mistake. If there was one thing BC knew how to do, it was how to make a dramatic comeback. After the Eagle defense got a big interception, Doug scored a touchdown on a running play. A field goal on the next drive cut the lead to 31–24.

By this time, the Alabama starters were back in the game. But BC had the momentum and kept rolling. With six minutes left, Doug threw a touchdown pass to fullback Jim Browne. The extra point tied the game.

Alabama was in shock. The Eagles got the ball back again, and Doug engineered yet another touchdown drive, giving BC a 38–31 lead. When Alabama couldn't score again, the game was over. A 17-point comeback on the road against a team as good as Alabama was stunning. The disappointed Alabama crowd could only watch in silence as Doug and his teammates celebrated the remarkable win.

❝Everywhere we play, the media wants to know about Doug. I tell the writers we have Brian Brennan here, a terrific receiver, has broken all the school records. The writers say, 'Fine, what time does Doug get here?' I say we have Steve DeOssie, a great linebacker, shaves his head, a true wild man. The writers say, 'Very interesting, now where's Doug?' That's just the way it is.❞

—REID OSLIN, BC SPORTS PUBLICITY DIRECTOR

The next game, against North Carolina, was one Doug had been looking forward to. In his freshman season, the Tar Heels had run up the score against BC in an embarrassing 56–14 blowout. Doug was eager to return the favor. He completely dominated the Tar Heel defense, hitting his receivers at will. He opened the game by completing each of his first twenty passes. The BC offense was unstoppable. Doug threw a school-record six touchdown passes in the game. Even more amazing, he did it in just over two quarters. Bicknell pulled his star quarterback out of the game early in the third quarter because the score was so lopsided.

In a little more than a half, Doug had gone 26 for 38 for 354 yards—probably his best game as an Eagle. It was a great way for Doug to stake his claim for the Heisman.

Doug struggled in the next two weeks, though, with a 24–10 win over Temple and a 21–20 loss to West Virginia. He rebounded with a win over Rutgers, which lifted the Eagles to a 5–1 record. The win set up another big rematch with Penn State.

The loss to West Virginia had seriously damaged BC's national championship hopes. A win over the Nittany Lions would go a long way to getting BC back into the mix. Doug did his part, completing 29 of 53 passes for 447 yards, but that wasn't enough. PSU held on for a 37–30 win, dropping BC's record to 5–2 and ending any remaining national championship chances. The dream of a New Year's Day bowl was still very much alive, however, as were Doug's Heisman hopes.

The Eagles couldn't afford any more losses. Doug and the Eagles beat Army in an offensive shootout, 45–31. During the game, Doug reached a personal milestone, becoming the first NCAA quarterback to ever throw for 10,000 career passing yards.

In the 1984 PSU game, Doug became the first player in NCAA history to gain 10,000 yards of total offense. Total offense is determined by adding together a player's total yards in passing, rushing (running), and receiving.

After a 24–16 Eagle win over Syracuse, Cotton Bowl officials had made up their minds—they wanted BC. The Cotton Bowl is one of the biggest college bowl games played on New Year's Day. The Eagles gladly accepted the invitation.

With that goal accomplished, Doug was eager to prove that the Eagles belonged in the Cotton Bowl. They still had two games to play in the regular season. The first was against Miami, where Doug threw the famous Hail Mary. His legendary comeback in that game erased all doubts and returned him to the status of Heisman frontrunner.

After "The Pass," the media demands on Doug were higher than ever. Everybody wanted to know about the little quarterback who had completed one of the most memorable passes in football history. So many reporters and TV shows wanted to talk to Doug that Bicknell finally cut them off. Enough was enough, he said. Doug still had one more regular-season game to prepare for. The coach didn't want his quarterback distracted any further.

December 1 was a big day for Doug. He started it by leading BC to a 45–10 victory over Holy Cross, giving the Eagles a final regular-season record of 9–2. The game was special for Doug because he threw a touchdown pass to his brother. After the game, the Eagles carried Doug off the field on their shoulders. Embarrassed, Doug begged the team to let him down.

Doug couldn't enjoy his normal postgame routine, though. After a quick shower and an interview with reporters, he was rushed to the airport and put on a flight to New York City for the Heisman ceremony.

Most fans and experts believed that Doug was a lock for the award. But Doug didn't want to get his hopes too high. "He's had his heart broken before," Joan Flutie said before the ceremony. "There have been other trophies he was going to receive, and they were given to someone else."

There was no disappointment this time. As expected, Doug was the winner. The other candidates—including Miami quarterback Bernie Kosar—shook Doug's hand as he stood to accept the award.

Doug was quite a story. Virtually unwanted by DI schools and considered too short to succeed, he had put together better statistics than any quarterback in NCAA history. The media and fans loved him. A week after the Heisman ceremony, he even visited President Ronald Reagan at the White House. It must have seemed like a dream. But the dream wasn't over yet. Doug and his Eagles had one more goal to achieve—to win the Cotton Bowl.

Doug had an important goal in his personal life too. On Christmas Day 1984, he asked Laurie to marry him. She quickly accepted, and the couple began to plan a summer wedding.

The next day, the Eagles flew to Dallas, Texas, to prepare for the Cotton Bowl. About 17,000 excited BC fans came to Dallas too. BC's opponent, the University of Houston, wasn't far from Dallas. But so many BC fans showed up that the Cotton Bowl almost felt like a home game for the Eagles.

The weather for the game was cold and windy. A steady rain fell, making it feel even colder. But if Doug was cold, it didn't show on the field. He threw three touchdown passes in the first half—a Cotton Bowl record—and led the Eagles to a dominating 31–7 lead. But his second half wasn't as good. He had a hard time gripping the ball in the rain. With Doug struggling, Houston charged back, cutting the lead to 31–28 in the fourth quarter.

"Doug looked a little dull in the eyes," Coach Bicknell later said. "That was because he was frustrated. He knows he's supposed to be great every game and it bugs him when he isn't."

A loss in that situation would have been a cruel way for Doug to end his college career. But he didn't let that happen. He led one last touchdown drive to seal the win. Doug's final touchdown pass went, appropriately, to Gerald Phelan. They'd come to BC together when the school was a football laughingstock. They left together as Cotton Bowl champions.

"If I had a choice between this and the Heisman, I wanted this," Doug said of the victory. "I'm happiest for this."

Chapter Four

The Next Level

Despite what many people had said, it looked like Doug would get his chance to play football professionally after all—but not necessarily in the NFL. The United States Football League (USFL) had started in 1983 to compete with the NFL, and its teams were interested in Doug.

The day after the Cotton Bowl, the USFL held its draft, and the New Jersey Generals selected Doug for their team. The selection meant that if Doug chose to play in the USFL, he had to play for New Jersey. Doug thought that an NFL team still might want him, but he'd have to wait for the NFL draft in April to find out.

NFL teams still weren't sure what to think of Doug. NFL scouts questioned his physical limitations. Would he be able to see over his own linemen? Would his body hold up under the punishment of NFL football? At the same time, scouts couldn't ignore Doug's remarkable college career. After all, he had won the Heisman Trophy as college football's best player. His career total of 10,579 passing yards was an NCAA record, and he'd gained most of those yards against quality competition. And because of his wide popularity, he would help any team sell tickets. Rumors about which team might pick Doug—and *when*—were the talk of the NFL.

> 66 *[Flutie is] the perfect college player, but that doesn't make him a great pro.* 99
> —NEW YORK GIANTS GENERAL MANAGER GEORGE YOUNG

Most of the rumors centered on the Buffalo Bills, who had the first overall pick in the draft. Many Buffalo fans desperately wanted the Bills to draft Doug. They even started a group called the Draft Doug Flutie Association. But for every supporter, there was a detractor. "I'd be a little afraid to pick him No. 1," said an official from one team. "Are you going to change your whole [plan] for this guy who's 5-9? When the time comes for the draft, there may be a lot of guys who excuse themselves to go to the restroom [so they don't have to make the decision]."

Meanwhile, New Jersey Generals owner Donald Trump was pushing hard to sign Doug. "Flutie represents a young, dynamic force," Trump said, adding that a big-name player like Doug would bring respect to the new league.

The money Trump was offering went up and up. When a Buffalo executive hinted that the Bills might not take him with the first pick, Doug made up his mind. He agreed to a six-year deal with the Generals worth $8.3 million. At the time, it was the largest professional sports contract ever paid to a first-year player.

DONALD TRUMP

Donald Trump is a businessman, billionaire, and celebrity. Born in New York in 1946, he made a fortune in real estate (buying and selling land and properties). He always liked side projects. The New Jersey franchise was one of his many businesses.

Trump's fame has grown since his USFL days. In 1996 he briefly ran for the Republican presidential nomination, and he considered running for the Reform Party nomination in 2000. Starting in 2004, he has produced and appeared in the hit television show *The Apprentice*.

Once the contract was signed, everything happened quickly. The USFL was set to play that spring (the league didn't play in the fall, so as not to compete directly with the NFL and the NCAA).

Doug wouldn't get much time off. The Generals traded their previous quarterback, Brian Sipe. It was Doug's team now.

Doug, meanwhile, enjoyed his newly earned fortune. He'd never had much money, so he delighted in buying a few luxuries, including his first car—a Porsche. He also spent money on the people he loved, including buying a new house for his parents. And he and Laurie could afford a nice wedding that summer and a comfortable house in the Boston area.

Generals coach Walt Michaels hurried to prepare his new quarterback. "There's only so many things we can do with a quarterback coming in late," he said. "We didn't know what he could do best and he had no idea about our system and what we were trying to do with a pro-style offense."

Doug quickly became friends with the team's other big-name star, running back Hershel Walker. Like Doug, Walker was a former Heisman winner who had been wanted by NFL and USFL teams alike. The two players formed a bond on and off the field.

The hype surrounding Doug's arrival was big. Trump and the USFL got exactly what they wanted—attention for the league. But expectations for the twenty-two-year-old quarterback were unrealistically high. Everyone realized that fact in the team's first exhibition (preseason) game, when his first three passes were intercepted.

A week later, the regular season started with a game against the Birmingham Stallions. Doug was nervous and it showed. His first nine passes fell incomplete, and the Generals went behind early. Doug's play improved later—he completed 12 of his last 18 passes—but his effort wasn't enough. Birmingham won the game 38–28.

> ❝Maybe [Doug] didn't have the physical stature of some of these perfect guys, but he had the ability to move the ball a lot better than them. You had some of these guys coming out that had all the physical attributes, that they could throw the ball 100 yards and everything else, but they didn't have his spirit.❞
>
> —DONALD TRUMP

For the second game, against the Orlando Renegades, the Generals tried a new strategy. Doug excelled late in games, when the offense is often in a hurry-up mode. In these situations, teams frequently run a "no-huddle" offense, in which the quarterback calls the plays at the line rather than in a huddle. New Jersey wanted to take advantage of Doug's skills and intelligence by running the no-huddle all the time. Opposing defenses would have trouble keeping up with Doug's frantic style, the coaches hoped.

The plan worked. Doug was on fire, completing three first-half touchdown passes and adding a fourth in the second half. The Generals won 28–10 and evened their record at 1–1.

Despite Doug's big day, the New Jersey offense centered on running, not passing. Doug's first job was to hand off the ball to Hershel Walker, the team's best player and main offensive weapon. Still, Doug had plenty of chances to throw the ball. In the third game—Doug's favorite of his USFL career—the Generals faced the Los Angeles Express before 58,000 New Jersey fans. Walker and Flutie ran over the Express defense. Doug scored three rushing touchdowns and added another through the air in the 35–24 win. His performance earned him the league's Player of the Week award.

But the season wasn't always easy. Doug was still learning a new offense. He struggled as the team lost two of the next three games, dropping its record to 3–3. Some fans complained about Doug's inconsistent play. They wondered how he could be Player of the Week one game and look completely lost the next. A 3–3 record wasn't good enough. If the Generals wanted to make the playoffs, they needed to play a lot better.

That's exactly what they did. Flutie and Walker led New Jersey to four straight wins. After the fourth, a reporter asked Doug if he'd been trying too hard earlier in the season. "I think a lot was expected of me," he answered. "Originally, the idea was to run Hershel and keep the heat off me, and try to get it going that way. . . . But we weren't running the ball early in the season. It just took a while to come together as a team."

66It's a great atmosphere here. When someone makes a big play, everyone's patting him on the back—whether it's an offensive player, a defensive player, or a field-goal kicker. We're a really together group, and . . . as the season goes on, we're coming closer and closer together.99

—DOUG FLUTIE ON THE NEW JERSEY GENERALS

All football players risk being injured. But for a scrambling, undersized quarterback like Doug, that risk is heightened. Because of his fearless style, Doug took a lot of hard hits from defenders twice his size. The constant pounding caught up with him in a June 1 game against the Memphis Showboats. Doug was running the ball in the first half when defensive lineman Reggie White caught him. As White drove Doug to the ground, Doug felt something snap. His collarbone was broken. His season was over. Without him, the Generals lost their first-round playoff game.

Doug's statistics in his rookie year weren't great. He'd completed 134 of 280 passes for 2,109 yards, throwing thirteen touchdowns and thirteen interceptions. He'd also run the ball for 460 yards and six touchdowns. In games he started, the Generals had gone 10–5.

In the summer of 1985, Doug watched with interest as the USFL fought to survive. Despite having stars like Doug Flutie, Hershel Walker, and Steve Young, the league was in financial trouble. It was also suing the NFL. It said that the NFL had a monopoly (didn't allow competition) in football and that it prevented TV networks from giving the USFL a television contract. The USFL needed TV money to stay in business.

It wasn't all bad news for Doug, though. That summer, he and Laurie finally married, after more than seven years of dating. About three hundred guests attended the wedding, held at Saint Patrick's Church in Natick.

The USFL-NFL lawsuit dragged on for months. USFL players, coaches, and fans didn't know whether the league would continue. Money troubles forced the Houston Gamblers to fold, and Houston merged with the Generals. The merger meant that Doug would have to compete with Houston star Jim Kelly for the quarterback job in the 1986 season.

The battle for the job never happened, though. A jury decided that the NFL did indeed have a monopoly. But in a surprising move, the jury awarded only $1 in damages to the USFL. The award sent a message that while the jury agreed with the USFL in the details of the case, it didn't believe the NFL should really be penalized. For all practical purposes, the USFL had lost. With the league prepared to fold, Trump agreed to let Doug out of his contract if he could find an NFL job.

Meanwhile, Doug waited. The Los Angeles Rams had drafted Doug in the NFL draft, even after he had signed with the USFL. The Rams had first dibs on him. But they didn't have much use for the small quarterback. As he waited, Doug worked out with his brother and the BC football team to keep in shape. He even briefly considered returning to school to play for the basketball team. Finally, on October 14, 1986—the last day before the NFL trading deadline—the Rams traded Doug's rights to the Chicago Bears. It was time for Doug to play football again.

Chapter Five

The NFL

Trading for Doug was a controversial move for the Bears, the defending Super Bowl champions. Several Bears, including star quarterback Jim McMahon, spoke out against the move. They didn't think the team needed the little quarterback. Doug hadn't even met his new team and already many in the locker room had turned against him.

Doug signed a contract with the Bears averaging about $125,000 per year. With few friendly faces among his teammates, Doug built a close friendship with Bears coach Mike Ditka. Ditka joked that the players threw tomatoes at him when he introduced the twenty-four-year-old quarterback. "Players get jealous," Ditka said. "They're very petty at times. I think that's what happened, especially when they saw I really embraced Doug. I embraced him because he's an outstanding person, as well as being a good football player."

IRON MIKE

Mike Ditka ("Iron Mike") is one of the most famous personalities in NFL history. He started his career as a player. In 1960 he was named the NFL's Rookie of the Year as a tight end for the Bears. He played in Chicago, Philadelphia, and Dallas before retiring in 1972.

Although he was an excellent player, many fans know him from his coaching years. He took over as the Bears head coach in 1982 and led the team to a Super Bowl title in 1986. He remained in Chicago until 1992 and coached the New Orleans Saints for several years in the late 1990s. After his coaching career, he went into football broadcasting.

Doug's first NFL game was November 9 against the Tampa Bay Buccaneers. Doug wasn't the starter, but he saw some action near the end of a 23–3 Bears win.

Two weeks later, McMahon injured his shoulder. Doug and Mike Tomczak shared the quarterback role the next week, again against Tampa Bay. In that game, Doug threw his first NFL touchdown pass. It went for 27 yards to future Hall-of-Fame running back Walter Payton. Doug added another touchdown on the ground (running) as the Bears cruised to a 48–14 victory.

But even that good performance wasn't enough to win over his teammates. Most of them believed that Tomczak should be the team's quarterback and that Ditka was showing favoritism toward the inexperienced Doug.

The next week—a Monday-night game against Detroit—the quarterback debate disappeared when Tomczak badly bruised his right leg. Doug still didn't know the entire offensive system, but he was the man. The game started slow. The Lions took a 6–3 lead into halftime. But late in the game, with the Bears trailing 13–9, Doug led a 74-yard touchdown drive for the win. The game wasn't great statistically—Doug went 13 for 24 for just 130 yards passing—but it was enough. "Thank God for the offensive line, for Walter Payton," Doug told reporters. "If they hadn't done it, we wouldn't have won the game. I didn't expect to struggle this much when I got my chance. I know I can do a lot better."

Doug's first NFL start came the next Sunday against Dallas. He threw two touchdown passes in a 24–10 Bears win. As in the previous week, Doug's stats were modest. But with such a good team around him, he didn't need to put up huge passing numbers. The Bears were built to win with running and defense, not a powerful passing attack.

Best of all, Doug was finally starting to earn the respect of his teammates. He'd proven that he could help the team win.

With McMahon and Tomczak hurt, the Bears needed him as they headed into the playoffs. Not everyone was convinced, though. McMahon continued to criticize Doug. He said that Doug wouldn't be able to cut it in the playoffs.

❝Today, I think Flutie gained whatever respect that he might have been lacking. You don't just come into a team and get respect and acceptance. . . . It's one thing to be a marvelous person and to throw a pretty spiral, but you've got to do it on the field. And Doug has and he did."

—BEARS LINEBACKER MIKE SINGLETARY, AFTER DOUG'S FIRST START WITH CHICAGO

Doug wanted to prove McMahon wrong in Chicago's first playoff game. The Bears were heavy favorites to beat the Washington Redskins. The game started out fine for Doug. He hit Willie Gault for a touchdown pass to take a 7–0 lead. But it all fell apart after that. Doug couldn't seem to do anything right, and the Redskins won 27–13. Doug went just 11 for 31 for 134 yards. "Things just weren't clicking today," he said. "I'll learn from it, but it wasn't a situation to go in and learn. It was a situation to go in and win."

With the Bears' season over, Ditka joked about Doug's struggles to learn the offense. In particular, Doug had had a hard time remembering the audibles—substitute plays that a quarterback makes at the line. "He'd call our audibles half the time, Boston College's half the time, and New Jersey's half the time," Ditka joked.

Despite Ditka's confidence in Doug, it was becoming clear that the undersized quarterback wasn't a part of the team's long-term plans. In the spring of 1987, the Bears drafted Jim Harbaugh with the idea that he would be the team's quarterback of the future. With that addition, Doug didn't have a real place on the team.

The 1987 season was one of strife for the NFL. The players' union went on strike (refused to play). The players wanted a better labor deal, including more money and better benefits and working conditions. Meanwhile, team owners hired replacement players to play the games.

During the strike, the New England Patriots wanted to trade for Doug. Knowing he had no future in Chicago, Doug wanted the trade too. Making the deal even better, Doug would be headed back to the Boston area, his home. But the Patriots had one condition before they'd make the trade—they wanted Doug to play for them even during strike games.

It was a difficult decision for Doug. As badly as he wanted the trade to go through, he didn't want to go against the players' union. But in the end, he agreed to New England's condition. The trade went through, and Doug played in one strike game before the dispute ended. The choice was controversial. Many NFL players were angry with Doug for not sticking with the union. They called him a scab, an insulting name for someone who takes the place of a striking worker.

Doug's start in the strike game was his only start of the season. When the regular players returned, he went to the bench. That's where he watched the rest of the Patriots' season.

Personally, 1988 was a big year for Doug and Laurie. They became parents when Laurie gave birth to a daughter, Alexa. Professionally, though, it was a tough year for Doug. He was buried deep on New England's depth chart as the third-string quarterback.

❝ *I play to the best of my ability. If that's not good enough, [then] it's not good enough. That's basically my attitude.* ❞

—DOUG FLUTIE

Many New England fans begged the coach to play the hometown hero, but Doug didn't see action until the season's fifth game. He came into the third quarter of a 7–7 game against the Indianapolis Colts. On his second drive, he led the Patriots 70 yards. He capped the drive with a touchdown pass to Stanley Morgan.

The Colts scored the next 10 points. With 2 minutes left, the Patriots trailed 17–14. But Boston football fans knew that this kind of situation was where Doug excelled. He didn't disappoint. Running the hurry-up offense, Doug went 6–6 on an 80-yard drive. He finished it by running the ball into the end zone for the winning touchdown. It was another classic Doug Flutie comeback. Despite playing less than a half, Doug was named the American Football Conference (AFC) Player of the Week.

After an embarrassing 45–3 loss to the Green Bay Packers, Doug and the Patriots beat the undefeated Cincinnati Bengals 23–20. That set up a big matchup with the powerful Chicago Bears. Doug badly wanted to beat the team that had given up on him. Before the game, McMahon taunted Doug through the media, calling him America's Midget.

Doug, eager to make a big impression, told his coaches that he wanted to throw a deep pass on New England's first offensive snap. He and wide receiver Irving Fryar had a play all set. The coaches agreed, and the plan was in place.

As Doug walked up to the line for that first play, everyone was ready. Doug snapped the ball and watched Fryar streak down the field. Doug stepped back and hurled the ball, hitting Fryar perfectly in stride. The wide receiver didn't stop running until he reached the end zone, 80 yards downfield. The Patriots celebrated as the New England crowd went wild. The big pass set the tone for the game. Doug threw three more touchdowns as the Patriots crushed the Bears, 30–7.

Ditka never liked to lose. But he admitted later that he took comfort in losing to his friend. "I wanted to say, 'I told you so [to the Bears],'" Ditka told reporters. "I didn't feel bad about getting my butt beat by [Doug]."

❝I think the little guy [Doug] is pretty special. I've thought that for a long time and the more he plays the more I know he's pretty special. He makes things happen. He's a winner.**❞**

—MIKE DITKA

Life was good. Doug wasn't putting up big numbers, but the Patriots won four of their next five games. The Boston fans and media were again in love with Doug. But New England coach Raymond Berry still wasn't convinced. The team was winning, but he thought Doug wasn't doing enough. With two regular-season games left, he decided to start Tony Eason instead of Doug. Doug was hurt by the decision, and many Patriot fans were angry.

Watching from the sidelines was difficult for Doug. Eason didn't have a good day in the first of the two games, but New England still won 10–7. In the last game, the Patriots played the Denver Broncos. A win would put them in the playoffs. If they lost, their season would be over.

Eason started the game but suffered an injury in the second half. Doug was ready to go in, but Berry went with Steve Grogan instead. The Patriots couldn't score with Grogan, and they lost the game 21–10. Doug got into the game at the very end to throw a Hail Mary, but even a touchdown reception wouldn't have been enough for a win. (The ball was intercepted.)

New England's season was over, and the fans were angry with Berry's decisions. Newspaper columnists blasted him. Fans vented their frustration on radio talk shows.

Despite an offer that spring from the Calgary Stampeders of the Canadian Football League, Doug returned to New England for the 1989 season. Again, he began the season as the third-string quarterback. But he earned a start in the team's fourth game, a 31–10 loss to Buffalo. After leading the Patriots to a 23–13 win over Houston, Doug hurt his ankle. The injury slowed him down and limited his ability to scramble. He played sparingly after the injury, ending another frustrating season on the bench.

After the season, the Patriots cut Doug from the team. The new head coach, Rod Rust, said that keeping Doug as the backup quarterback would never work. The Boston fans liked Doug too much, Rust said. They'd never give the first-string quarterback a fair chance.

By this time, it was clear. Doug's NFL career was going nowhere. It was time for a change.

Chapter Six

A New Brand of Football

With his NFL career stalled and the USFL out of business, Doug looked north for his next opportunity. Ever since college, people had said that his skills would be a perfect fit for the Canadian Football League (CFL). CFL football is not the same as NFL football. The rules are a little different. The field is wider and the end zones are much larger. These features favor fast, scrambling quarterbacks like Doug.

Doug began talks with the British Columbia Lions. The Lions had lots of talent at quarterback already, but a star like Doug would be a valuable addition. After a long negotiation, Doug agreed to a two-year contract that would pay him $350,000 per year. It wasn't a very big contract compared to NFL (or USFL) standards, but it was the richest deal in CFL history.

Murray Pezim, the Lions' owner, was excited about his new superstar. But the other CFL owners were concerned.

As a student at Boston College, Doug Flutie (#22) became one of the most famous college football players in the nation when he threw a 48-yard touchdown pass in the last seconds of a 1984 game against the Miami Hurricanes. Here, he celebrates the win as a teammate carries him.

Doug Flutie won the 1984 Heisman Trophy. The Heisman goes to the most outstanding college football player in the United States. No other Boston College player has ever won this award.

Doug Flutie *(left)* and Herschel Walker *(right)* played together on the New Jersey Generals in 1985. This team was part of the short-lived United States Football League (USFL).

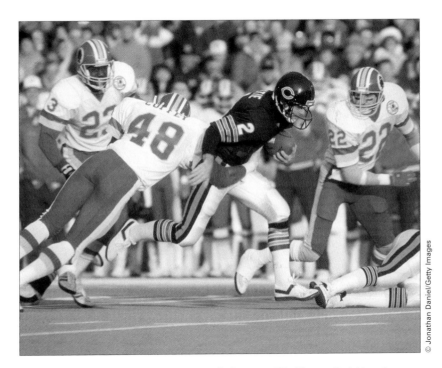

Playing for the Chicago Bears, Doug Flutie (#2) dodges Washington Redskins players during a 1986 divisional playoff game.

In 1990 Doug Flutie (#2) left the NFL to join the Canadian Football League (CFL). He played for several teams, including the Toronto Argonauts.

Doug spent the final years of his career—1998 to 2005—back in the NFL. In this 1999 game, he led the Buffalo Bills to victory over the New England Patriots.

Flutie Flakes is a breakfast cereal named for Doug Flutie. It was first sold in 1998, when he was a member of the Buffalo Bills. A fan brought this box to a November 1, 1998, game between the Bills and the Miami Dolphins.

On January 1, 2006, Doug Flutie became the first football player in sixty-four years to successfully dropkick an extra point after a touchdown. Playing for the New England Patriots, he helped them defeat the Miami Dolphins. It was Doug's final professional football game.

Doug Flutie *(right)* speaks with reporters in Washington, D.C., about his support for autism research. Doug's son, Dougie, was diagnosed with autism, a disorder that affects the brain.

AP Photo/Tyler Mallory

© Getty Images

Doug and his wife, Laurie, attend the 2006 ESPY Awards in Hollywood, California. Even though he retired from professional football that year, Doug remains a fan favorite.

The CFL wasn't a big business like the NFL. It didn't have a rich TV deal. Its games didn't sell out huge stadiums. Most owners couldn't afford to pay the kind of money Doug was getting.

The CFL season, which begins in the summer, was quickly approaching. Pezim was eager to see Doug in action. A week and a half after he signed, Doug was in uniform for an exhibition game in Winnipeg. A crowd of 34,000—a CFL record for an exhibition game—filled the stadium to see the new star.

Doug entered the game in the second half. He quickly noticed the differences in the league's style of play. He had lots of room to scramble and buy time for his receivers. He completed 8 of 15 passes for 102 yards. He also ran for 61 yards and scored two rushing touchdowns. Doug soon realized that in the CFL, his legs were almost as important a weapon as his arm.

As the 1990 regular season approached, the excitement about the Lions grew. Ticket sales soared. On July 13, Doug finally made his regular-season debut. With the Lions trailing 27–15, he entered the game. Just as he'd done his whole career, he led a comeback, highlighted by a Hail Mary touchdown pass to end the first half. The game ended in a 38–38 tie.

Despite his impressive debut, 1990 was really just a learning experience for Doug. He had to get used to the new rules and style of play in the CFL. "I'm still coming into form," he said of his inconsistent play that season. "The game is still so new, every day I feel something different. I'm just scratching the surface. Believe me, it will come."

FORGIVEN AT LAST

One of Doug's British Columbia teammates, Ian Sinclair, had been on the Miami Hurricanes when Doug beat them with his famous Hail Mary pass in 1984. After Doug joined British Columbia, Ian joked with reporters that he wouldn't forgive Doug for 1984 until he threw a Hail Mary for the Lions. Doug did just that in his first game with the Lions.

It was a tough year for British Columbia. With a losing record, Pezim made a midseason coaching change, firing Larry Kuharich and replacing him with Jim Young. The Lions finished with a record of 6–11–1. Doug completed 209 of 392 passes that season. He threw for sixteen touchdowns but was intercepted nineteen times.

Doug entered the 1991 season with new energy and optimism. It wasn't just about football either. Shortly before the season, he and Laurie learned that they were going to become parents again. They both eagerly awaited the end of the year, when the baby was due.

Lions fans were also optimistic, and with good reason. With Young as the coach and with Doug having a year of experience, the team was poised for a big season. Almost every game was close, including an amazing six overtime contests. Doug put up huge statistics and was as confident as he'd been since his days at Boston College.

One of 1991's most memorable games came against the undefeated Toronto Argonauts. Toronto was the league's best team. It had several big-name players, including 1990 Heisman runner-up Raghib "Rocket" Ismail. The game was a tight offensive shootout that went into overtime. A crowd of more than 52,000 watched Doug lead the Lions to a thrilling 52–41 victory. Beating the powerful Argonauts was a big hurdle for the Lions. With the win, they felt confident they could compete for the Grey Cup, the CFL's championship trophy.

A few weeks later, Doug was up to his old tricks. With less than a minute left, the Lions trailed the Saskatchewan Roughriders 47–36. Doug led two quick drives, throwing one touchdown pass, then running for the winning score. Doug later wrote that the 50–47 win was probably the most amazing comeback of his career. In the game, he went 37 for 50 for 478 yards and five passing touchdowns.

A few weeks later, Darren Flutie joined the Lions as a wide receiver. He'd recently been cut by the NFL's Phoenix Cardinals.

In his first game with British Columbia, Darren caught three passes from Doug for 63 yards. Darren quickly became Doug's favorite target. "When he got in the game, I was the one who got [nervous]," Doug wrote. "It was just like that in college. I wanted to get him the ball."

In a 45–38 loss to Edmonton, Doug broke Warren Moon's CFL record of 5,676 passing yards in a season. By the end of the season, Doug had added nearly another 1,000 yards to the record, finishing with an amazing 6,619. He hadn't just broken the record—he'd shattered it.

For the season, he completed 64 percent of his passes and threw thirty-eight touchdown passes (he rushed for fourteen more touchdowns). He was named the league's Most Outstanding Player, the CFL's version of the MVP award. Behind Doug's remarkable season, the Lions posted an 11–7 record and earned a playoff berth.

The Lions, the CFL's highest-scoring team in 1991, traveled to Calgary, Alberta, for a first-round playoff game. Despite holding a 31–15 lead at halftime, the Lions couldn't hang on. Calgary's offense was almost unstoppable in the second half. The Stampeders surged to a 43–41 win. British Columbia's season was over. "Doug carried us through that game," Darren Flutie said. "We scored 41 points, and basically he did that all on his own. I felt really bad for him."

With such an amazing season, the twenty-eight-year-old Doug was in high demand. He had offers from NFL teams as well as a huge offer from the Calgary Stampeders. Doug didn't want to leave British Columbia. He liked the organization and loved playing with his brother. But Pezim couldn't afford him anymore. He couldn't pay even close to what the other teams were offering Doug.

Doug decided that Calgary was the best fit. He still had dreams of playing and starting in the NFL. But in the CFL, he was a huge superstar, and that is where he'd stay. He signed with Calgary for a reported million dollars per season. Team owner Larry Ryckman, excited about his new star, said Doug was the Wayne Gretzky (hockey's greatest player) of football.

Doug's life was changing off the field as well. In November 1991, Laurie gave birth to Doug Flutie Jr. The couple was thrilled. With two children to support, Doug was more determined than ever to earn his big salary in Calgary.

Proving his worth wouldn't be easy. His record-breaking 1991 season had set almost impossibly high standards. In addition, he was joining a Stampeder team that had reached the Grey Cup championship game the year before. The fans expected great things of the team and its new quarterback.

Calgary started the season with a win and a personal milestone for Doug. He went over 10,000 passing yards in his CFL career—by far the fastest any player had reached that mark. The team followed the first game with another win. Doug was showing that he was worth the big contract.

"Over the first two games, we got a flavor of what Doug was truly about," said Calgary receiver Dave Sapunjis. "All of a sudden there was an excitement generated around the team because we knew the opportunity was there not only to be a great team but to win the Grey Cup that year."

The next game was big for Doug personally. The Stampeders played British Columbia in their home stadium in Vancouver. Doug and the Stampeders handily beat his old team—and his brother—37–19. Next came a 28–26 comeback win over Toronto. The win pushed Calgary's record to 4–0. The Stampeders couldn't hold on to that momentum, though. They lost three of their next four games, despite good numbers from Doug.

The streaking Stampeders rebounded, winning four of the next five games, with Doug breaking one team passing record after the next. The highlight of the streak was a 57–29 victory over Winnipeg. It was the highest point total in Calgary Stampeders history. The team finished the year with a 13–5 record. Doug totaled 5,945 yards on the season. He also rushed for 669 yards, a personal high.

Calgary's playoff opponent for the Western Division Finals was the Edmonton Eskimos, a team that had beaten the

Stampeders during the regular season. It was a bitterly cold game. Gusts of wind tore across the field, making it difficult to pass the ball. Doug ran all over the field, using his legs to make plays. He led Calgary to a slim second-half lead, but Edmonton fought back to take the lead, 22–16.

Doug and the offense took the field with just 1:18 left in the game. Everyone knew Doug's reputation for comebacks, so the excitement in the stadium was high. After a first-down pass, the ball was near midfield. Then Doug dropped back and unloaded a long pass to wide receiver Allen Pitts, who was tackled at the Edmonton 15-yard line. Doug ran for 8 yards on the next play. With the fierce wind, he didn't want to risk throwing a game-ending interception. So he ran it again, this time for 5 yards.

The ball was at the 2-yard line, and less than 20 seconds remained on the clock. In the huddle, Doug desperately tried to put on his shoe, which had come off when he'd been tackled on the previous play. But the clock was running and he didn't have time. He jammed his foot in the best he could, snapped the ball, and took off running. The shoe came flying off, but that didn't stop him. The one-shoed quarterback dove into the end zone for the game-winning touchdown. Calgary was going to the Grey Cup championship game!

"When you look at great players in the history of sports, when the big games are on the line, they usually step up," said

Calgary coach Wally Buono. "I don't think Doug in any way was going to be denied now that he was so close. . . . You knew he was going to put it in the end zone."

An Unexplained Injury

The night after the Stampeders won the 1992 Western Division Finals, Doug's foot started to hurt. One of the joints was locked in place—he couldn't move it. He soaked the foot in water. He tried everything to get the joint moving again. Finally, he rubbed a spot that popped. The joint was unlocked. The next day, he saw the team's medical staff, but nobody could explain what had happened.

Calgary's Grey Cup opponent was Winnipeg. The Blue Bombers had posted an 11–7 record during the regular season. For some reason, the Winnipeg coaches chose not to tailor their defense to stop Doug's special talents. Instead, they ran their normal defensive sets. Time after time, Doug made them pay for the decision. It was Doug's first chance to perform in a championship game, and he shone. Before coming out of the game in the fourth quarter, he threw for 480 yards and built Calgary a big lead. The Stampeders used mostly backups to finish out the 24–10 victory.

Doug and his teammates were the CFL champions. It almost seemed strange to win so easily. Doug was known for thrilling comeback wins, not comfortable victories. But Calgary's fans weren't complaining. Doug's performance earned him the Grey Cup MVP award and proved that he was worth every dollar of his big contract.

Professionally, Doug was a champion and the two-time CFL Most Outstanding Player. Personally, he had a wife and two children that he adored. He spent his free time listening to and playing music. Life, it seemed, couldn't get much better.

Chapter Seven

CFL Ups and Downs

Doug's success in Calgary continued in 1993. On the field, he did everything that could be expected of him. He led the Stampeders to a 10–0 start, and they finished the season with a league-best 15–3 record. He threw for 6,092 yards and forty-four touchdowns in the regular season. He added another eleven touchdowns on the ground—numbers that earned him another Most Outstanding Player award. More important, he led Calgary to another Grey Cup title game. But the Stampeders lost the game, which was played in brutal cold (-44 degrees Fahrenheit by game's end).

The loss shouldn't have overshadowed all Doug had done for the team. Yet Calgary owner Larry Ryckman told reporters that he'd wasted a million dollars on Doug. The comment stung Doug, who had done nothing but work hard. Worse still, reporters suggested that his hands had frozen in the Grey Cup championship game, when his team needed him most. People said he couldn't win in cold weather, even though he'd been doing it for years. The 1993 season had been spectacular except for one game, yet Doug felt terrible about it.

The news at home in Boston, however, was far worse. Doug Jr.—nicknamed Dougie—had in his first few years seemed like a normal baby and toddler. He learned new words, put them together in phrases, and then spoke short sentences. But in 1994, Doug and Laurie noticed Dougie regressing. He talked less and less. He stopped using sentences. Soon, he was back to using single words to communicate. Before long, he stopped talking altogether.

Doctors diagnosed Dougie's problem. He had a condition called childhood disintegrative disorder (CDD), a form of autism. Autism is a brain disorder that hinders a person's ability to interact and communicate with others. The news was crushing for Doug and Laurie. The son they had known had practically disappeared. Worse still, there was no known cure.

"When we first learned Dougie had autism, we thought, 'What do you mean, autism? We can't have a child that has a problem,'" Doug and Laurie wrote. "But after a while, you learn that it could be much worse. You have to think that it's really not that bad—Dougie is great. At first, it was hard to take, but we have to accept Dougie for who he is. He always has a smile on his face, and when he walks into a room, he brings a smile to your own face. He has many qualities about him that are special."

Dougie's struggles made Doug's problems with the Stampeders seem minor by comparison. He returned for the 1994 season and dominated, just as he had for the past three seasons. Calgary's offense was so potent that many opponents criticized them for running up the score unnecessarily, such as on August 25, when Calgary crushed Toronto 52–3.

Argonauts president Bob Nicholson watched the blowout. "[Doug] just scrambled and threw," he said. "He was just incredible. I just watched the whole game and I had to swallow my pride. . . . I just shook my head at the time and said, 'This is one guy we've just got to get here in Toronto.'"

Despite his football success, Doug lists his favorite sport as basketball. His favorite athlete, however, was a baseball player—former Baltimore Orioles shortstop Cal Ripkin Jr.

Again, Doug led the Stampeders to a 15–3 record. He threw for 5,726 yards and a CFL record forty-eight touchdowns. Statistically, it was another amazing year. Again, Doug was the league's Most Outstanding Player.

Calgary opened the playoffs by crushing Saskatchewan 36–3. In the next game, they faced the British Columbia Lions and Darren Flutie. Doug and the Stampeder offense were still on fire, but so was the Lions' offense. Neither defense seemed able to make a stop. Late in the game, Calgary held a 5-point lead, but they missed a field goal to give British Columbia a shot at the win. The Lions had the ball with the clock running out. It was an unusual feeling for Doug. He could only watch as an opponent drove down the field in a comeback attempt. He was helpless on the sidelines.

British Columbia moved the ball steadily. With 15 seconds left, they were at the Calgary 25-yard line. On the next play, Darren Flutie made a diving catch at the 5-yard line. With time left for just one play, quarterback Danny Mac snapped the ball, avoided the Calgary rush, and found Darren in the end zone for the game-winning touchdown.

Once again, Calgary had put together the league's best regular-season record and had nothing to show for it. Doug was happy for Darren. But losing still hurt.

The next season, 1995, would be one of the most miserable seasons of Doug's career. At home, he and Laurie continued to learn about how to raise an autistic child. On the field, nothing went right. From early in the season, Doug's right elbow was stiff and sore. Before long, the pain affected his passing. He threw mainly short passes and avoided long, hard throws. During one game, the elbow hurt so much that he told his coaches to put in backup quarterback Jeff Garcia.

At first, doctors couldn't find anything wrong with the elbow. They just told Doug to rest it. Garcia took over as the starter while Doug tried to heal. But when the elbow didn't get any better, he went back for more tests. This time, the doctors found the problem. The tendon in Doug's elbow was torn.

Doug had surgery to repair the injury. The surgery was a success, but the doctors said he would need six months to heal. Doug was crushed—sitting out six months would end his season. Garcia was a good quarterback, but Doug hated the idea of letting down his teammates. He was determined to come back sooner.

While he did his rehab (exercises to heal the elbow), Doug did all he could to stay busy and keep his head in the game. He worked with the coaches to make game plans. He helped broadcast a game between Calgary and Toronto on TV. He even played wide receiver for the Stampeders' scout team (practice players who help starters prepare for games). Playing as a wide receiver allowed Doug to be on the field without risking his elbow. All the while, Doug hoped to make it back before the season was over. Calgary wasn't dominating as they had in previous years, but Garcia kept them in the playoff hunt.

Doug's elbow healed faster than doctors had expected. Soon, he was well enough to begin light throwing. Slowly, he pushed the elbow harder and harder. By the team's final regular-season game, he was ready to test it. He played a little against Toronto, completing eleven of sixteen passes. His elbow had passed the test. He was ready to play in Calgary's first play-off game, against the Hamilton Tiger-Cats.

Despite the encouraging signs, Doug still wasn't 100 percent confident in the elbow, and it showed. He was terrible in the first half and told Coach Wally Buono to put in Garcia for the second half. Garcia struggled as well, but Calgary's defense had a good game. The Stampeders held on for the win.

The coach gave Doug another shot in the next round against Edmonton. This time, Doug was much sharper. On the first drive, he went 5–5 and led the Stampeders to a touchdown. He continued to throw and run well. Calgary had a 30-point lead by halftime. Buono pulled him out of the game for the second half—his work was done. The Stampeders were headed to the Grey Cup title game.

Their Grey Cup opponent was the Baltimore Stallions. Baltimore was part of a three-year CFL experiment to include teams based in the United States. The U.S. teams had a big advantage. They didn't have to conform to an old CFL rule requiring a certain number of a team's players to be Canadians.

Because the United States had a larger pool of talented football players, the Stallions were a deeper, stronger team.

Making Doug's job even tougher was the brutal weather. The wind was so strong that officials considered postponing the game. They let it continue, and the teams played a close, hard-fought contest. Baltimore pulled away late in the second half for a 37–20 win. Doug later admitted that the Stallions were simply the better team. Without the Canadian restriction, their roster was much stronger.

After the loss, Doug's relationship with Stampeders owner Larry Ryckman got worse. Ryckman had money troubles. He couldn't pay Doug's salary. The paychecks got later and later and soon didn't come at all. With Dougie's special needs at home, a steady paycheck was more important than ever. As time passed, it became clear that Doug wouldn't be returning to Calgary for the 1996 season. The CFL declared Doug a free agent. He could sign with any team of his choice.

> ❝I have had the chance to be Doug's teammate and he's an incredible athlete and a great person. When Doug decides to retire, he will be remembered as one of the greatest players to grace the CFL.❞
> —OFFENSIVE LINEMAN ROCCO ROMANO

Toronto, Edmonton, and British Columbia all wanted to sign him, and he briefly considered a return to the NFL. But he ended up signing a two-year deal with the Argonauts.

The Argos, traditionally one of the CFL's best teams, had been terrible in 1995. They had stumbled to a 4–14 record and were eager to get better. The coaches gave Doug more offensive control than he'd ever had in football. He had a huge say in how the offense would operate and which kinds of plays it would run.

The decision paid off for Toronto. In the first game, Doug led a comeback drive capped by a touchdown pass to wide receiver Paul Masotti with just 14 seconds left. "Everyone felt that [Doug] was going to get a touchdown and we were going to win the game," said Argo coach Don Matthews. "There was just an amazing confidence that came from everybody, [starting] from him. . . . It was the Flutie magic that he does whenever he steps on the football field. He just has that ability that when the game's on the line, somehow he finds a way to win."

The Argos won 27–24, and the turnaround had begun. They won seven of their next eight games. Excitement about the team was as high as ever. Doug enjoyed being appreciated. For the first time in a couple of years, he was having fun playing football.

After two more wins, the hot streak finally ended with a 35–11 loss to British Columbia. That set up a big game with

Calgary—a clash between the CFL's two division leaders. It was strange for Doug to play against his old team. He was eager to show the Stampeders what they were missing.

The Argos fell behind early, but Doug led them back in the second half. By the fourth quarter, Toronto held a 20–13 lead. Doug didn't let up. He threw a 97-yard touchdown pass to Masotti that sealed the victory.

Toronto just kept winning and clinched first place in the Eastern Division. They ended the season at 15–3—the best record in the league. Doug threw for 5,720 yards and twenty-nine touchdowns and was again the league's Most Outstanding Player. But that didn't matter much to Doug. He wanted a championship. That was what mattered.

Toronto dominated the Montreal Alouettes in the Eastern Division Finals. After a late touchdown in the blowout, the coaches let Doug have some fun by kicking an extra point. Doug admitted that the kick was weak, but it went through. It was a unique way for Doug and his teammates to celebrate the win and their trip to the Grey Cup title game.

Toronto's Grey Cup opponent, the Edmonton Eskimos, was led by the league's best defense. It was also Darren Flutie's new team. The matchup between the Flutie brothers was the big story in the media before the game. "They built it up so much that the brothers were playing against each other," Doug said. "It was a good experience. For both of us to play in such a big game like that with the whole season riding on it, that was special."

ANOTHER FLUTIE IN THE RECORD BOOKS

Doug wasn't the only Flutie setting CFL records. While Doug was smashing the league's passing records, Darren was doing the same to its receiving records. Over his twelve-year CFL career, he caught 972 passes, more than any CFL receiver in history. He also set the record for most playoff receptions with eighty-five and tied Allen Pitts's record of nine seasons of 1,000 or more receiving yards.

As usual, the game took place in cold, windy conditions. Critics still said Doug couldn't play in the cold, and he hoped to finally quiet them. The Eskimos pulled ahead to an early lead, 9–0. The Argo offense didn't move well and committed turnovers. Doug focused on the run instead of the pass. Suddenly, the offense found its groove. Soon, both offenses were clicking and taking turns scoring. The lead passed back and forth.

With three minutes to go, the Argos had a 3-point lead and the ball. Doug just needed to take care of the ball and keep the clock moving. With short, safe passes and runs, that's exactly what he did. Toronto held on for the win. After four years, Doug was once again a Grey Cup champion.

After the game, the thirty-four-year-old quarterback angrily told reporters that he'd heard enough about him not being able to win in cold weather. "I've played some of my best games in the playoffs in bad weather," he said.

No CFL team had won back-to-back championships in twenty-five years. In 1997 Doug and the Argos were set to change that. The team got off to another strong start, despite a nagging toe injury on Doug's right foot. He played through the pain, and Toronto was again atop the Eastern Division standings. Doug's body continued to take a beating, though. A hamstring injury slowed him down even more and caused him to miss some playing time. Still, the team was dominant and finished the season 15–3—again the best record in the CFL.

Doug was sick with the flu the week before the Eastern Division Finals against Montreal. Laurie came up from Boston to help nurse him to health. By game time, he was still weak.

The game started off slowly, but Doug overcame his illness and played well. Late in the fourth quarter, Montreal kicked a field goal to tie the game at 30. Doug and the offense took the field. Doug was just hoping to drive for the winning field goal. But then, he dropped back to pass and found Mike "Pinball" Clemons downfield. Clemons caught the perfect pass, spun away from his defender, and ran for a game-clinching 58-yard touchdown. The Argos were headed back to the Grey Cup.

Their opponent was the surprising Saskatchewan Roughriders. The Roughriders had finished the regular season with a losing record. But they'd still managed to squeak into the playoffs in the weak Western Division. They had gone on to win two very close playoff games to advance to the Grey Cup.

In 1998 a Canadian rock band called Moxy Früvous wrote a song about Doug. "Doug Flutie Song" poked fun at Doug's small size but also showed that he was a hero to many Canadians.

There was no doubt which was the better team, and it didn't take long to prove on the field. With a good defense and a ball-controlling offense, the Argos jumped out to a 27–9 half-time lead. By the time the game was over, Toronto had a 47–23 victory and a second straight championship. Once again, Doug was the game's Most Outstanding Player.

Doug Flutie was a three-time CFL champion and a six-time Most Outstanding Player. By far, he was the most dominating player the league had ever seen.

Chapter | Eight

Another Comeback

Doug's two-year contract with Toronto was completed. He was once again a free agent. With two titles in Toronto, he felt he'd accomplished all he could in the CFL. It was time to return to the United States. Doug was ready to give the NFL another shot.

A handful of teams were interested, including New Orleans, coached by Mike Ditka. But Buffalo was the most serious. They offered only $250,000 for the year—a lot less than Doug had been making in the CFL. The money wasn't the main factor in Doug's decision. He still believed he could be a successful NFL quarterback, and he wanted the chance to prove it. He signed the deal and packed his bags for Buffalo.

"I came back from Canada with a fresh new outlook and really didn't care what [critics] thought as much," Doug said. "At that point, it was all gravy. I felt, honestly, at thirty-five years

80

old, I was ready to retire and decided, oh, let's give it a shot, two more years."

The Bills had gone 6–10 in 1997 and were in a period of change. They had a new head coach in Wade Phillips. Their longtime quarterback, Jim Kelly, had recently retired after leading the team to four Super Bowls. (Unfortunately, the Bills lost all four.) Buffalo fans didn't know what to expect from their team, and they certainly didn't know what to expect from a 5-foot-9, thirty-five-year-old quarterback.

❝It's a great opportunity for [Doug] up there. . . . He's meant to go to Buffalo. I hope they win a Super Bowl.❞

—MIKE DITKA

The media didn't know what to think about the signing either. The *Buffalo News* called the move a mistake and a possible embarrassment for the team. But many fans were excited. They'd wanted Doug in a Buffalo uniform since before the 1985 draft.

The starting job wasn't Doug's, though. The Bills had traded for Rob Johnson, a promising young quarterback. Johnson had never been an NFL starter, but Buffalo had him penciled in as their number-one guy. His hold on the job only got stronger when Doug struggled in the preseason.

BILLS HISTORY

The Buffalo Bills played their first season in 1960 as part of the American Football League (AFL), which later merged with the NFL. The Bills won AFL championships in 1964 and 1965, but they have not won a league championship since that time. The team name comes from Buffalo Bill, a performer who toured Europe and the United States with his Wild West show in the late 1800s.

When Johnson got hurt in the first regular-season game, Doug got his shot. It was the third quarter, and the Bills trailed the San Diego Chargers 10–0. The situation was a familiar one for Doug. He calmly led the Bills offense to two touchdowns—both on passes to wide receiver Andre Reed. In the final minute, he led his team downfield and gave kicker Steve Christie a shot at a 39-yard field goal for the win. Christie missed the kick, however, and the Chargers held on for the victory.

Despite Doug's strong performance, Johnson returned to the starter's role the next week. Doug didn't get significant playing time again until Johnson was hurt in the fifth game against the Indianapolis Colts. Doug was fabulous in the game, throwing two touchdowns and completing 23 of 28 passes. He led the Bills to a second-half comeback and a

31–24 win. For his performance, he was named the NFL's Player of the Week. "Doug was fantastic," said Coach Phillips. "He hit every pass, it looked like. The ones he didn't [complete] were on the money. He's a winner and made all the big plays we needed him to do today."

In 1998 Doug and Laurie formed the Doug Flutie Jr. Foundation for Autism. The foundation has raised more than $7 million. Most of the money goes to help autistic children and their families.

Suddenly, Doug was the talk of Buffalo. The fans loved him. Even the media sang his praises. A few months earlier, Doug had agreed to lend his name and image to a breakfast cereal called Flutie Flakes. With Doug's success against Indianapolis, sales of the cereal skyrocketed. Some of the profits went to the Doug Flutie Jr. Foundation, a charity that Doug and Laurie had started to help children with autism.

Johnson was still banged up the next week for a game against the Jacksonville Jaguars, so Doug got the start. Once again, he and the Bills needed a comeback. Down 6 points with two minutes to play, Doug led the offense on a 70-yard touchdown drive. The highlight of the drive was a 39-yard pass to Eric Moulds that put the ball on the 1-yard line.

After spiking the ball to stop the clock, Doug tried two passes. Both fell incomplete. It was fourth down. The Bills had to score or the game was over. Doug snapped the ball, but the play fell apart. The running back, confused about the play, failed to take the handoff as planned. Left holding the ball, Doug did the only thing he could—he ran. The confused Jaguar defense never touched him as he scampered into the end zone. With the extra point, the Bills took the lead and won the game. It was yet another example of the Flutie magic.

Johnson continued to suffer with his injury, so Doug remained the starter. He kept the momentum rolling with a win over the Carolina Panthers, highlighted by an 82-yard touchdown pass to Moulds. With each game, more and more people became fascinated with Doug's story. For years, nearly all the NFL executives had agreed that Doug wasn't suited for the league. Once again, Doug proved his critics wrong. The Buffalo offense had been stale under Johnson. With Doug, it was dangerous and dynamic. Opponents' defenses struggled to contain the scrambling quarterback with the wide-open style.

Meanwhile, Phillips insisted that Johnson would return as the starter once he was healthy. No matter what he did, Doug was still the backup. But Johnson wasn't healthy yet, so the offense was still Doug's to run. A victory over division-rival Miami continued the success. The team, 1–3 when Doug took over as the starter, was by then 5–3 and in the playoff hunt.

ROB JOHNSON

When the Bills traded for Rob Johnson in 1998, they thought they were getting an up-and-coming superstar. The former University of Southern California quarterback had spent three years as a backup with the Jacksonville Jaguars. With Jacksonville, he'd started just one game and thrown only two career touchdown passes. After moving to Buffalo, Johnson never emerged as a starting-caliber NFL quarterback. After four disappointing seasons in Buffalo, he moved on to serve as a backup for the Buccaneers and the Giants.

As good as things were on the field, Doug and Laurie suffered heartbreak off it. Laurie had been pregnant with the couple's third child, but she lost the baby in a miscarriage. Doug had been looking forward to becoming a father again, but it wasn't to be. Instead, he focused on football.

As the Bills kept winning, the pressure on Phillips grew. The fans and media demanded that he leave Doug in the starting role. And it was impossible to ignore the results on the field. No quarterback in the league was playing better. Finally, Phillips gave in and announced that even when Johnson was healthy, Doug would remain the starter.

In 1998 Doug completed his autobiography with the help of sportswriter Perry Lefko. The book, titled *Flutie*, tells Doug's life story from his birth to his decision to return to the NFL.

A few weeks later, Doug returned to New England for a showdown with the Patriots. The game was a huge story for the loyal fans in Boston. They still loved Doug and gave him a warm welcome. One sign in the crowd showed the fans' split support. It read, Doug: Best of Luck. But Not Today.

By halftime, New England had a 14–6 lead. But Patriots fans knew that with Doug Flutie in the game, the lead wasn't safe. In the second half, Doug and Moulds connected for an 84-yard touchdown pass—the longest of Doug's NFL career.

A strange fourth quarter followed. With a 21–17 lead, the Bills appeared to have the game won. But a bad call from an official gave the Patriots a first down on a ball caught out-of-bounds. Next, New England threw a Hail Mary. This time, an official called pass interference—a rare call on a Hail Mary. The Bills thought the official was wrong. The call gave the Patriots another chance. They scored to take the lead and win the game.

It was a tough loss for Buffalo's players, coaches, and fans, who felt the officials had robbed them of a victory. "It's a shame for our team because they played their hearts out," Phillips said of the questionable calls.

The Bills bounced back with a win over the Bengals. Doug was still playing well, and the playoffs were within reach—something not expected of the team before the season started. Two weeks later, the Bills clinched that playoff spot. After a 1–3 start under Johnson, they had finished the regular season at 10–6.

Doug was showered with honors for his performance. He was voted to the Pro Bowl (the NFL's all-star game). He was also named the NFL's Man of the Year and the Comeback Player of the Year. The individual honors were nice, but Doug's focus was on the playoffs. He'd never won a playoff game as an NFL starter.

In the first round of the playoffs, the Bills faced the Dolphins. The game began as a defensive struggle. A 32-yard pass from Doug to Moulds tied it midway through the third quarter. The Bills appeared to take the lead late in the fourth quarter, but a questionable call wiped out the score. Still, the

Bills had a shot late. Down by 7, Doug led the offense downfield for a final drive. With a mix of long passes, short passes, and runs, he took the Bills deep into Miami territory as the clock ticked down. With 17 seconds left, Doug ran the ball to Miami's 5-yard line and called Buffalo's final time-out. But on the next play, Doug was sacked. He never saw the defender coming, and he fumbled the ball. Miami fell on it, gaining possession. The game—and Buffalo's season—was over.

It wasn't the finish Bills fans had been hoping for. But Doug was finally a force in the NFL. Doug used his renewed fame and all the publicity to increase awareness about autism and to raise money for Dougie's autism foundation.

Chapter Nine

Final Seasons

In 1999 Doug finally entered an NFL season as the starting quarterback. After a loss to Indianapolis in the first game, Doug led the Bills to four straight wins. The team had a good defense, and with Doug leading the way, the offense moved the ball well.

The team kept winning. One of the highlights of the season came in a cold, windy, December 26 game against the Patriots. The Bills entered the game at 9–5 and needed a win to ensure a playoff spot. With the bad weather, neither offense could do much. With less than five minutes to play, the Bills trailed 10–3. That's when Doug led the team on a 59-yard touchdown drive, completing every pass he threw. With the extra point, the game was tied at 10 and headed into overtime.

Buffalo got the ball to start overtime, and once again they looked to Doug to lead them down the field. Doug picked up where he had left off in the fourth quarter. He completed one short pass after another. Soon he had the Bills inside the Patriots' 20-yard line. Kicker Steve Christie came in for a short field goal to end the game. When the ball sailed through the uprights, the team rushed onto the field to celebrate yet another Doug Flutie comeback. "Doug had a heck of a game," said Coach Phillips. "He made . . . a lot of big plays running and, all of a sudden, he got hot throwing the football."

Doug Flutie was one of many CFL players to move to the NFL with success. Others on the list include Warren Moon, Jeff Garcia, Rocket Ismail, and Mike Vanderjagt.

The Bills' playoff spot was secure, so the team rested many of its starters for the final game against first-place Indianapolis. Rob Johnson was among the backups who got a chance to play. Johnson was fantastic in the game, leading the Bills to a 31–7 victory. Statistically, it was the best game a Bills quarterback had had all season. Suddenly, the quarterback controversy was back on.

Phillips had to make a decision quickly. The team was set to play the Tennessee Titans in the first round of the playoffs. Doug hadn't had a great year statistically, but the team had gone

10–5 in his starts. Still, Phillips decided to go with Johnson in the playoffs. It was a controversial move. Reporters blasted the decision, and many fans were furious. When the Titans beat the Bills 22–16 on a last-second kickoff return for a touchdown, the criticism only grew.

"I honestly believe that if I would have been playing, we could have, would have, won," Doug later said. "It probably was the most frustrating, most miserable week I've ever spent in football. It was hard to understand and difficult to deal with."

Doug Flutie is one of only seven professional football players to throw for more than 50,000 yards. Adding his totals from the USFL, CFL, and NFL, he has thrown for 58,179 yards.

Adding to Doug's frustration was his age. He was thirty-seven years old. He knew his time as a starter was quickly running out.

In 2000 Doug's playing time dropped. Once again, he and Johnson shuffled in and out of the starter's role. Neither quarterback was able to really get going, and the team struggled to an 8–8 record. One of the season's few highlights came in a 16–13 overtime victory over the Patriots. With less than two minutes to play, Doug led a drive to tie the game, then won it in overtime.

But overall, it was a difficult season for Doug and the team. He was ready for a change. Before the 2001 season, he signed a contract with the San Diego Chargers. San Diego had gone 1–15 the year before, so Doug knew the team wasn't a playoff contender. But he also knew he'd be starting there, which wasn't the case in Buffalo. He'd also be helping guide rookie Drew Brees, San Diego's quarterback of the future.

Doug started all sixteen Chargers games in 2001. While the team started out 3–0, it quickly faded and finished with a 5–11 record. That was an improvement over the miserable 2000 season, and Doug was a big part of that turnaround. He threw for a career-high 3,464 yards. But 2001 was also one of the most forgettable seasons of his career. Doug had never been on a truly bad team before.

Doug's role in 2002 changed significantly. His years as a starter were behind him. After a year of sitting and learning, Brees was ready to be San Diego's number-one quarterback. Even though he struggled, the Chargers wanted to give him as much experience as possible. Doug played in just one game that year.

Doug returned to the Chargers in 2003 and 2004 in a similar role. He was there to help Brees progress. Still, he did start a few games. In 2003, at age forty-one, he became the oldest NFL player to rush for two touchdowns in a single game. He was also the oldest player to win an AFC Offensive Player of the Week award. But the highlights were few and far between. By 2005 he was ready to head home to Boston. He signed with the Patriots as a backup to Tom Brady.

 After retiring from the CFL in 2002, Darren Flutie took a job with CBC, the Canadian TV network.

He knew that 2005 would be his final season in football. As expected, Doug saw little action that year. It was nice to retire as a Patriot, though. After all, Doug had made his name in Boston.

Late in the year, Doug found an unusual way to end his career. In the final regular-season game, against Miami, Brady led the team to a touchdown. Normally, the placekicker comes in to kick the extra point. But an old NFL rule also allows a player to score the extra point with a dropkick—a ball that's dropped and touches the ground before it's kicked. Nobody had used a dropkick since 1941. It's a risky play because footballs aren't as round as they used to be. A dropped ball can easily take a funny bounce.

Coach Bill Belichick had seen Doug trying dropkicks in practice. For fun, he decided to let Doug dropkick the extra point. The Patriots had already clinched a playoff spot, so it didn't matter if Doug messed up. The Miami coaches and the fans were confused when the play started. "I couldn't figure out what was going on," said Dolphins coach Nick Saban. "They had a quarterback in, four tight ends, and a receiver and there was no kicker."

 After the 2005 season, Doug briefly considered playing one final year for the Argos in the CFL. According to Darren Flutie, Doug decided against the comeback, unsure that his body would stand up to an entire CFL season.

Saban figured it out soon enough. Doug snapped the ball, calmly dropped it, and kicked it just as it touched the ground. The ball sailed through the uprights for the extra point. This was the last time Doug stepped on an NFL field as a player.

One of a Kind

In May 2006, Doug Flutie announced his retirement. The announcement brought a formal end to a fascinating and unique career. For more than twenty years, Doug Flutie was the quarterback who defied expectations. At one level after another, he proved his critics wrong by excelling. By scrambling and thinking on his feet, he overcame the problems associated with his small size. He dominated at the high school and college levels and starred in three professional football leagues.

Even after retirement, Doug wasn't done with football. At the press conference announcing his retirement, he told of plans to pursue a career in broadcasting. He signed a three-year contract with the ABC and ESPN television networks to work as a host for college football broadcasts. This new career will give Doug a chance to put his education and his speech communications degree to use. And the break between seasons will allow him to spend more time with Laurie and his children, especially Dougie, who needs extra care and attention. Doug will also have more time to play in the Flutie Brothers Band, which performs shows for charity.

Shortly after Doug's retirement, a debate in the media raged. Does Doug Flutie belong in the Pro Football Hall of Fame? Almost all the Hall of Famers are former NFL stars, but Doug spent his prime years in the CFL. Many argue that Doug was so dominant in the CFL that he deserves a spot in the hall. Others discount his CFL statistics. They say the CFL is so far below the NFL in terms of talent that the stats are meaningless. Time will tell whether Doug is inducted into the hall. Players must be retired for five years before they even become eligible. (Doug is certain to be inducted into the CFL Hall of Fame, however.)

No matter how the debate ends, there's no debate about one thing: Doug Flutie's career was one of a kind. There will always be underdogs, but there will never be another story quite like Doug Flutie's.

PERSONAL STATISTICS

Name:

Douglas Richard Flutie

Born:

October 23, 1962

Height:

5'9" (often listed as 5'10")

Weight:

180 lbs.

Throws:

Right-handed

CAREER STATISTICS

USFL							
Year	Team	Games	Att	Comp	Yards	TD	Int
1985	NJ	15	281	134	2,109	13	14

NFL							
Year	Team	Games	Att	Comp	Yards	TD	Int
1986	CHI	4	46	23	361	3	2
1987	NE	2	25	15	199	1	0
1988	NE	11	179	92	1,150	8	10
1989	NE	5	91	36	493	2	4
1998	BUF	13	354	202	2,711	20	11
1999	BUF	15	478	264	3,171	19	16
2000	BUF	11	231	132	1,700	8	3
2001	SD	16	521	294	3,464	15	18
2002	SD	1	11	3	64	0	0
2003	SD	7	167	91	1,097	9	4
2004	SD	2	38	20	276	1	0
2005	NE	5	10	5	29	0	0
NFL totals		92	2,151	1,177	14,715	86	68

CFL

Year	Team	Games	Att	Comp	Yards	TD	Int
1990	BC	16	392	207	2,960	16	19
1991	BC	18	730	466	6,619	38	24
1992	CAL	18	688	396	5,945	32	30
1993	CAL	18	703	416	6,092	44	17
1994	CAL	18	659	403	5,726	48	19
1995	CAL	11	332	223	2,788	16	5
1996	TOR	18	677	434	5,720	29	17
1997	TOR	18	673	430	5,505	47	24
CFL totals		135	4,854	2,975	41,355	270	155

Key: **Att**: attempts; **Comp**: completions; **TD**: touchdowns; **Int**: interceptions

GLOSSARY

audible: a change in the play call. Quarterbacks call audibles as they get ready to snap the ball, depending on the position of the defense.

autism: a brain disorder that hinders a person's ability to communicate and interact with others

blitz: a defensive play in which defenders who don't usually rush the quarterback do so

concussion: a bruise to the brain

draft: a system for selecting new players for professional sports teams

free agent: a player who isn't currently under a contract and is free to sign with any team

monopoly: control over an entire industry by one business or company. The USFL accused the NFL of having a monopoly on football, saying the NFL unfairly pushed out competition.

scholarship: money given to a student to help pay the costs of schooling

strike: a walkout by a group of workers. Workers strike in an attempt to get higher wages, better working conditions, or more benefits.

SOURCES

4 Ian Thomsen, *Flutie!* (Chester, CN: Globe Pequot Press, 1985), 122.
4 Ibid.
6 Barbara Siegel and Scott Siegel, *Doug Flutie* (New York: Avon Superstars, 1985), 8.
7–8 Thomsen, *Flutie!* 20.
8–9 Siegel and Siegel, *Doug Flutie*, 10.
10 Ibid., 12.
10–11 Doug Flutie, *Flutie* (Champaign, IL: Sports Publishing., 1999), 7.
12 Thomsen, *Flutie!* 21.
14 Flutie, *Flutie*, 11.
15 Thomsen, *Flutie!* 25.
16 Ibid., 25.
17 Ibid., 32.
18 Flutie, *Flutie*, 17.
18–19 Siegel and Siegel, *Doug Flutie*, 25.
21 Thomsen, *Flutie!* 34.
22 Ibid., 44.
26 Siegel and Siegel, *Doug Flutie*, 33.
28 Thomsen, *Flutie!* 90.
28 Siegel and Siegel, *Doug Flutie*, 35.
30 Thomsen, *Flutie!* 101.
31 Flutie, *Flutie*, 26.
32 Thomsen, *Flutie!* 106.
32 Ibid., 109.
33 Ibid., 98.
36 Ibid., 132.
38 Ibid., 137.
38 Ibid., 138.
40 Kris Schwartz, "Hail Flutie," *ESPN.com*, 2006, http://sports.espn.go.com/espn/classic/bio/news/story?page=Flutie_Doug (April 13, 2006).
40 Flutie, *Flutie*, 41.
40–41 Siegel and Siegel, *Doug Flutie*, 47.
42 Flutie, *Flutie*, 48.
43 Ibid., 45.
44 Siegel and Siegel, *Doug Flutie*, 51.
45 Ibid., *Doug Flutie*, 51.
48 Flutie, *Flutie*, 63.
50 Ibid., 65.
51 Ibid., 67.
51 Ibid., 68.
52 Robert Mcg. Thomas Jr. and Thomas Rogers, "Scouting; Triple Threat," *New York Times*, March 24, 1987, http://query.nytimes.com/

gst/fullpage.html?res=9B0DE6DE11 3EF937A15750C0A961948260 (May 1, 2006).
53 Perry Lefko, "Flutie CFL's Outstanding Player," *Toronto Sun*, November 22, 1996, http://www.canoe.ca/96GreyCup/nov22_awards.html (May 20, 2006).
55 Flutie, *Flutie*, 76.
55 Ibid., 67.
59–60 Ibid., 90.
62 Ibid., 95.
62 Ibid., 98.
64 Ibid., 103.
65–66 Ibid., 110.
69–70 "Dougie's Team," *The Doug Flutie Jr. Foundation*, http://www.dougflutiejrfoundation.org/dougiesteam.html (May 10, 2006).
70 Flutie, *Flutie*, 121.
74 "Doug Flutie—ArgoHeros," *Toronto Argonauts*, http://argonauts.ca/Argos/History/ArgoHeroes/2004/09/20/636820.html (May 10, 2006).
75 Flutie, *Flutie*, 154.
76–77 Ibid., 166.
78 Canadian Press, "Flutie, Vanderjagt Receive Honors," *Canoe*, November 24, 1996, http://www.canoe.ca/96GreyCup/nov24_mvp.html (May 20, 2006).
80–81 Howard Ulman, "Flutie Ends 21-Year Pro Career, *Yahoo Sports*, May 16, 2006, http://sports.yahoo.com/nfl/news?slug=ap-flutieretires&prov=ap&type=lgns (May 20, 2006).
81 Flutie, *Flutie*, 197.
83 "NFL Recap (Buffalo-Indianapolis)," *CNN/SI.com*, October 11, 1998, http://sportsillustrated.cnn.com/football/nfl/scoreboards/1998/10/11/recap.indianapolis.buffalo.html (June 19, 2006).
86 Flutie, *Flutie*, 224.
90 Associated Press, "OT Win Puts Bills in Driver's Seat," *ESPN.com*, December 26, 1999, http://espn.go.com/nfl/1999/991226/recap/bufnwe.html (July 6, 2006).

91 "Doug Flutie's Ongoing Bitterness over Being Benched," *Profootballweekly.com,* February 24, 2000, http://archive.profootballweekly.com/content/archives/features_1999/spin_022400.asp (July 6, 2006).

94 "Flutie Converts First Drop Kick Since 1941 Championship," *ESPN.com,* January 2, 2006, http://sports.espn.go.com/nfl/news/story?id=2277308 (July 9, 2006).

BIBLIOGRAPHY

Flutie, Doug. *Flutie.* With Perry Lefko. Champaign, IL: Sports Publishing, 1999.

Mandell, Ted. *Heart Stoppers and Hail Marys: 100 of the Greatest College Football Finishes (1970–1999).* South Bend, IN: Diamond Communications, 2000.

Siegel, Barbara, and Scott Siegel. *Doug Flutie.* New York: Avon Superstars, 1985.

Thomsen, Ian. *Flutie!* Chester, CN: Globe Pequot Press, 1985.

WEBSITES

CFL.ca Network—Official Site of the Canadian Football League

http://www.cfl.ca

The CFL's official site includes news, scores, standings, a CFL rule book, and more.

The Doug Flutie Jr. Foundation for Autism, Inc.

http://www.dougflutiejrfoundation.org

The website of Doug Jr.'s autism foundation includes information and resources for autistic people and their families, as well as information about Doug Jr. and his father.

ESPN.com—Doug Flutie

http://sports.espn.go.com/nfl/players/content?statsId=443

ESPN.com's player page on Doug includes vital statistics, career passing and rushing statistics, and feature articles.

NFL.com—The Official Site of the National Football League

http://www.nfl.com

The NFL's official site includes scores, news, statistics, video features, and other information for football fans.

INDEX

HPARX +
B
F647D

DOEDEN, MATT
    DOUG FLUTIE

PARK PLACE
12/07